EMO

ENERGY IN MOTION

Silvia Hartmann

2016

DragonRising

Publishing

EMO Energy In Motion

© Silvia Hartmann 2016

ISBN: 978-1-908269-86-7

Second Edition, v2016

Published by
DragonRising
United Kingdom
DragonRising.com

Other titles by this author:

Energy EFT
Events Psychology
Infinite Creativity
Modern Stress Management: The Trillion Dollar Stress Solution

WELCOME BY SILVIA HARTMANN

Welcome to EMO: Energy In Motion.

In this book, you will find a new way of living, working and playing with energy.

The purpose of EMO is to give us a simple set of skills and tools we can use to lead happier lives.

EMO is the first downright logical, practical, sensible and testable approach to conceptualising energy of the new millennium.

Originally created to be a primary research tool for modern energists, it was found that EMO was the key to profound and lasting energy healing for the energy body.

EMO does a whole lot more than "just healing" however.

EMO is all about feeling better.

Feeling happier, brighter, more energized, more joyful, more often.

The name EMO comes from setting energy in motion - moving energy. This means practically to be gaining the ability to do something to stop feeling sad, angry, depressed and so forth, to improve the energy flow, and as a result, to feel better and experience not just peace or relief, but actually happiness where once there was misery.

When we – as normal people – feel well, feel bright, energized and lively, we work much better in every way possible.

We work better, we play better, and being friendly, compassionate and loving comes easy because we have plenty of energy and lots to give to others, from attention to physical assistance and everything in between.

In fact you could say that if more people were happier, more often, we would have less war, crime, and sickness all around, and the human world would be a far better place.

EMO is designed to make people happier, and thus to set them free to be able to do more things they enjoy, make more of a contribution to others, and lead happier lives – without having to join a cult, believe in anything, or follow any guru of any kind.

So let us start now with the basics and ask, "How does EMO make people happier? How does that work?"

PART 1 – EMO, EMOTIONS & ENERGY

Emotions Come From The Energy Body

We asked the question, "What are emotions?"

The answer we found was that emotions are movements in the human energy body which can be felt through the physical body, thus producing a very real "feeling."

We feel sad, and we feel happy.

These are by no means just words or turns of phrase; that's exactly the case with emotions, that we feel things that seem to have no physical cause.

Whether these feelings are small and light, easily overlooked like a shiver going down your spine when you enter a building that has "a peculiar atmosphere" or whether these feelings are extreme, such as feeling as though your heart is breaking with physical stabbing pains in the chest when a loved one has died, there is always a physical sensation that is what we call an emotion.

And so it turns out that it is the energy body and the movements and happenings in the energy body that cause us to feel emotions.

All Emotions Are Movements In The Energy Body

Now, this simple but profound statement unlocks the understanding of emotions, and all by itself heals many, many ills that have plagued us humans for thousands of years.

People have emotions, but they don't understand them; they are scared of them, don't know how to handle their emotions, or what to do to feel differently.

When people have extreme emotions, caused directly by extreme injuries in the energy body, as you would find with someone who was sexually abused as a child, was tortured, shot or raped, for example, they used to think that they were crazy or mad.

13

This then causes a second level of emotions, and a third as we start to ask why are we mad, doesn't God love us, do I deserve to suffer, which cause even further stress, and all the talking in the world cannot resolve this, and things get more and more out of control.

We say to a person who has experienced the frightening reality of emotions, the very real pain and the disturbed thinking they produce,

> **"No, you are not crazy to feel all these uncontrollable emotions.**
>
> **"These emotions, these sensations are real and they have a good reason for being there.**
>
> **"Emotions are designed to tell us what goes on in the energy system.**
>
> **"Emotions are the feedback system for the energy body, just as physical pain is the feedback system for the physical body.**
>
> **"All that is wrong with you is that your energy body was hurt at some time, and it was never treated, never repaired properly.**
>
> **"You are neither mad, nor crazy, and when your injuries have been treated, you will find that you can experience different types of emotions instead of all that pain.**
>
> **"You can feel the joy and happiness of being alive again.**
>
> **"This is possible, it is doable, and we can show you how you can do this too."**

Without any treatment, this simple truth makes a huge difference.

Remember this when you are dealing with other people, and with yourself:

Extreme emotions = extreme injuries in the energy system.

14

This is not esoteric, or a matter of faith.

It is simply a fact.

The injuries in the energy body translate directly across to the emotions, the sensations a person experiences; there is nothing complicated about it, it is simple and direct.

The location of the physical sensation that is the emotion is the exact place where the disturbance in the energy system is located.

For example, if someone tells us that they just got fired and felt "as though they had been punched in the stomach" the injury is located exactly there – in the stomach.

When someone feels pain in their chest after a bereavement, then the injury in the energy system is in their chest.

When someone holds their head as they cry, "I'm going mad!" the injury or disturbance is located in the head – it really is as simple as that.

The disturbance is located exactly where the emotion is felt.

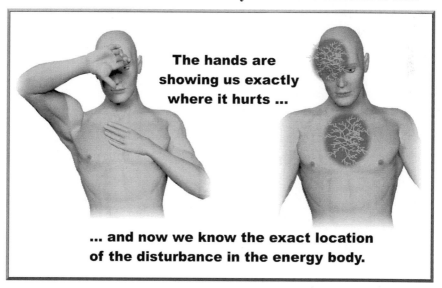

The hands are showing us exactly where it hurts ...

... and now we know the exact location of the disturbance in the energy body.

Let us take a moment now to review these simple, basic facts.

To many people, it is shocking that these simple cause-and-effect connections have not been revealed before, and that is absolutely extraordinary, it is true.

What I would like you to note at this point is that knowing these few facts changes the way we approach all forms of emotional healing, and all forms of treatment for emotional disturbances profoundly.

It changes the way we think of other people as we begin to understand why they behave the way they do.

It also changes the way we start to think of ourselves, our self concept.

Most importantly, understanding the relationship between disturbances in the energy system, the corresponding emotions this produces, and how in the past, we have consciously misunderstood and misinterpreted what that means, opens the door to a brand new pathway out of the old suffering, and into a new world altogether where we really can be happier – and it is surprisingly easy.

So to sum up this first and most important chapter of all, here it is one more time.

- **The human energy body transmits information about its condition through body sensations that have no physical origin – emotions and feelings.**

- **The body sensations correspond directly to the places in the energy body where these energy movements take place.**

- **ALL human emotions are information about the movement of energy in the energy body.**

From this simple observation now flows a whole range of new ways of dealing with human emotions, which are the direct cause of thought and behaviour in human beings.

You change the emotions, and you change everything.

As a result, working with EMO and human emotions, in therapy and personal development for example, has different strategies compared to what went before.

This essential difference weaves its way through every aspect of working with energy and emotions so that people get to feel less pain, then no pain at all as we approach the "zero point of peace" but then we go beyond and into the range of positive emotions, which tell us when the energy system is working well, and into pleasure and joy of being alive.

The first major difference in EMO is that we do not label emotions or use emotional words.

"It Is ONLY An Energy ..."

We have become used to – or you could say, conditioned into – using a great many words and labels to describe how we feel. There are all the straightforward labels for emotions such as,

- – I am angry.
- – I am sad.
- – I am disappointed.
- – I am ashamed.
- – I am feeling anxious.
- – I'm depressed.
- – I hate him.

… and so on and so forth.

This can spiral out of control as we have emotions about having emotions, leading to such unfortunate things as,

- – I feel appalled at being disgusted with myself for being so angry.
- – I can't forgive myself for failing to forgive the people I hate.
- – I'm ashamed at my inability to stop feeling so anxious all the time and that makes me really depressed.

... and so on and so forth.

Then, there are the metaphorical descriptions and labels, such as,

- – My heart is breaking.
- – He stabbed me in the back.
- – I felt like I was punched in the stomach.
- – He ripped my heart out.
- – I am drowning in an ocean of despair …

… and so on and so forth.

This is the normal way people describe their emotional states.

What we have to remember, and learn to remember, is to think to ourselves every time we hear someone using such labels for the feelings in their body that at the end of the day,

"It's only an energy movement in the energy body."

or for short,

"It's only an energy."

In EMO, it really doesn't matter what the emotional problem may be or how it has been previously labelled.

We direct attention to the place where the problem is located in the energy body by responding with, **"Where do you feel this** (guilt, anger, sadness, burden, misery, depression, anxiety, guilt, shame, terror, disgust, dislike, hatred, grief, attention seeking deficit etc. etc. etc.) **in your body?**

"Show me with your hands."

Now, we know where the problem is located. We have something to look at, something to focus on, something real to work with.

And it is wonderful to say to someone who has been struggling with emotional pain, or even psychosomatic pain or phantom pain, and who has been told that "it's all in their heads" or accused of "just making it up" to finally realise that …

- Yes! There really is "something" there that is causing this.
- No! You didn't imagine it, you didn't make it up.
- No! You're not crazy!
- No! It's not "all in your head"!
- Yes! I believe you are in real pain.
- Yes! You can show us where it hurts you.
- Yes! Now we know where the disturbance lies, we can **treat this**.
- Yes - you can feel better.

By not talking about emotions, or using labels or words or metaphors or pop psychology terms, and instead, immediately locating the place of disturbance in that one person's energy body, we open the door to actually handling what was wrong in the first place.

By not talking "about emotions" we also don't have to talk about:

- What happened how, where and when;
- Who did what to whom;
- Whose fault it was;
- If it did or didn't really happen;
- Why it happened;
- What it means;
- If there was a purpose;
- If it would be better to stay in pain;
- What would happen if this ever got healed;
- What wouldn't happen if it did or didn't get healed;
- And what any of it might or might not mean.

We are focusing on the central place of disturbance that is calling out for help by generating these emotions, just as your foot would call out for help using physical feedback when you have stepped on a rusty nail.

In the absence of an understanding what emotions are, where they come from or how to treat them, people have talked in circles and tried to make meaning of their suffering and of their experiences which included finding all sorts of reasons why it was somehow good or right for them to suffer.

I hope you can understand that this doesn't help anyone, and that there is no merit in delaying treatment, or "taking it easy" or worrying about ecology, or drawing out any treatment for emotional pain, injuries and disturbances unnecessarily.

We are simply dealing with something that needs healing, and that should be healed as quickly as possible.

By focusing on the place of the disturbance or injury, we are "putting to rights what once went wrong" and help the person feel better as soon as possible.

So one of the core rules of EMO is:

Don't talk "about" emotions.
Focus on the real body sensations
and work with there really is.

Remember:

No matter what the old labels were,

"This is ONLY energy."

This is the direct path to healing painful emotions, and then beyond healing into feeling much, much better as the energy body comes to life.

Energy First!

To begin with, it is sometimes difficult to tell the difference between a powerful negative emotion, a psychosomatic pain, a phantom pain and a physical pain.

EMO deals only with healing the energy body and alleviating energy based pain, not with physical pain or physical sickness of any kind.

So how are we to know whether a pain is an energy pain or a physical pain that needs the attention of a physician rather than an energy healer?

The answer is simple - if in doubt, put **energy first**.

EMO costs nothing and takes only a few moments.

If the experience of pain has an emotional or energetic component, it will respond to the EMO treatment and sensations will change.

This is going to lead at the very least to less stress on the entire mind, body, energy body system and that is always good thing.

Whatever is left can then be dealt with in a physical way.

This is very easy to do, easy to remember and works for all different kinds of manifestations and problems.

No matter what the problem may be, put energy first. It doesn't hurt, can only help and will help us decide if other treatments are necessary after the fact.

Energy First!

The Basic Rules Of Energy

Energy is a natural occurrence that we might not be able to see, or hear, or currently measure, but we can sense energy.

We have a 6th sense which are the sensations in our body.

This is how we feel, how we "feel emotions."

Our 6th sense is an internal diagnostic to tell us about the state of our energy body, and it is also an external connector to sense energy occurrences at large.

In EMO, we don't go any further to define what energy might or might not be; we follow some simple principles which hold true for all things in nature, so we may presume these also hold true for energy occurrences.

These basic rules of energy are as follows.

Energy must flow.

There is never anything stuck in nature; all natural systems have a flow, an evolution, a forward momentum and an absolute future orientation. When we encourage stuck energy to start to flow, we are moving in the right direction.

Every energy form has a perfect place in time & space.

When you take something out of its natural context, chaos ensues; and a rose in a herb garden becomes a weed, and vice versa. We may therefore presume that all energy forms we can ever encounter likewise have a rightful place for them somewhere in the general ecology of the energy worlds, and if we can let them go to where they belong, they will cease to cause trouble.

There is only energy and the absence of energy.

People make judgements based on what feels good and what feels bad. There is no such thing as bad energy - there is only energy, which feels good, and the absence of energy, which feels bad. Treating all energy experiences as **only energy** helps with staying calm and logical and assists working with energy correctly at any level.

Energy is normal, natural, and absolutely everywhere.

People all have energy bodies and they all have the capacity to feel energy in their own body through their 6th sense, that of the body sensations which have no physical origin. We are designed and constructed to live and play as energy beings in the Oceans of Energy. To increase our energy awareness is not just entirely natural, but the right thing to do.

If you keep these basic rules of energy in mind at all times, the invisible but sensible worlds of energy stop being spooky, freaky and scary, and instead become perfectly logical, natural and easy to deal with.

The Energy System

In the past, people made many maps of the human energy body.

There were spirals and lines and endless points, and none of it can be made visible by the technology we have today as it stands.

And it is true that the human energy body is a very complex system.

However, we do not need to worry about mapping the whole human energy system, or learn standard models with 42,000 different nadis or a million different acupuncture points.

When we work with EMO to change people's emotions from negative to positive, we simply work with **what is really there**.

If you remember, we said earlier that if we tell someone whose chest hurts badly because they are in emotional pain that they're not actually hallucinating, or crazy, or making it up, but that there really something there that causes this pain, people take a huge sigh of relief and say, "Thank God! Finally someone believes me, finally someone understands!"

In EMO we call something made from energy that is really there (and not any kind of imagination, hallucination, make belief, madness etc.) an EREA.

- **EREA is short for "Existing Energetic Reality".**

It means that there is something really there, and it is made from energy, and we know its location.

That is all we know about it, and for EMO, that is all we need to know.

The person in front of us has a disturbance in their chest, they show us with their hands where the disturbance is located, and so here, we have an erea.

By not distracting ourselves with thoughts "about" this erea, whether it is a nadi or a meridian, a chakra or some kind of demonic possession, or a spirit attachment, or any kind of unhelpful metaphor imaginable, we get to focus on what there really is – and that's probably the very first time ever this erea has received such focus of attention from either their owner, or from a healer, for that matter.

- **In EMO, we deal with one erea at a time.**

We give it our undivided attention, and this is the very first step to have an impact on the energy body.

At the same time, and because we are finally stepping away from ideas, words and metaphors and extend all our senses to discover what is really there, what is really happening, right here, right now, with this one completely unique person, we are also learning something about the human energy body, how it works, what it needs – every time we pay with attention, we literally get rewarded with new information in return.

Over time, this will build up a new way of "reading the energy system" - your own, and that of others. The important concept is that an energy system has to be read here and now, in real time, as it is – and not as an ancient map might decree that it should be.

Every person on Earth looks different, and different people have different fingerprints.

The energy system is much, much more fluent than that, and even identical twins have vastly different energy systems that you could never mistake for one another.

This is wonderful, and exciting; and some people's energy systems are much more "individualised" than others, because of the experiences, good and bad, that they had somewhere along the line.

By only and ever dealing with what's right there in front of you, or happening inside of you as the case may be, and laying aside all thoughts of idealised templates of what there should be (but actually isn't!) the effectiveness of energy work takes a quantum leap – even in the hands, or should I say, the healing hands of a complete beginner.

This is very important to understand and remember about the theory and practice of EMO, so here are the main points once more.

The Energy System In Brief

1. Every person has an absolutely unique energy system and no map has ever been drawn of that one unique energy system.

2. In EMO, we lay aside all ideas of old maps and labels, and focus on what is really there – the existing energetic reality, that which the person feels in their body.

3. By paying attention to what is really there, right here, right now, we make the first important connection through which energy and information streams between ourselves and the erea we are going to be treating and healing.

4. By treating what is there, right here, right now, we can never go wrong or lose our way in the complexities of the energy system.

5. Over time, we learn to "read energy" in a whole new way – fluently, in real time, and extremely accurately.

Using The Energy Body To Heal The Energy Body

When we start to think about healing the energy body, it is natural to say, "How on Earth am I supposed to do that? I can't even see it, it's so complicated, it's so other than – where do you start?"

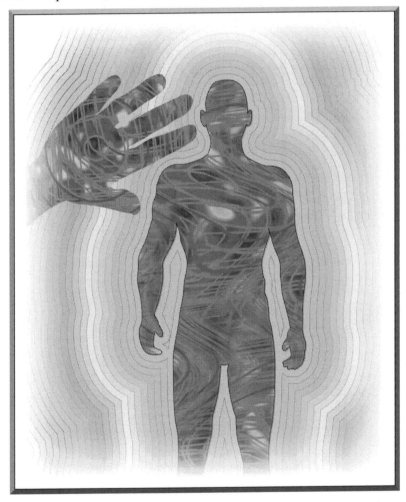

Where we start is with the simple and delightful observation that **we all have an energy body each.**

Most people don't actually know this, but even the people who have done energy work for decades sometimes fail to understand the very practical nature of that energy body we all have.

Very simply put, our energy body has "reflections" of the physical body, but they're made of energy rather than of material matter.

So our energy body has, for example, energy arms, and energy hands.

These energy hands are the "healing hands" we've heard so much about.

These energy hands of energy that everyone owns affect the energy system of another person, or your own, because they're made of the same stuff and function on exactly that level.

It is really very simple; and once you know this, it becomes natural and obvious to shift your attention from your "flesh hands" to your hands of energy, which activates them and brings them to life, lets them know that we want them to do something (at last!).

The next stumbling block is as follows.

"Ok, so I have these healing hands of energy. But what do I do with them? What do I tell them to? I don't know how they work, or what they should be doing?"

That's fair enough, and quite right.

"We" as in our conscious minds who are reading and writing this, "we" really don't know what to do.

But there is a part of us who does.

Our energy body does not just have hands, and organs, and rivers and streams through which energy flows, and power centres and connectors; it also has a head.

And this "energy head" is **the energy mind** – a brain that is made from energy, works with energy, and also has receptors like energy

31

eyes, energy ears and energy feelers that let it know what's going on in the energy world.

Previously known as the "unconscious mind" or "subconscious mind," the energy mind is who knows what to do because it can see, hear and feel exactly what's going on in its own or another person's energy system, and it also knows how to do things there, and how to do them right.

What we have to do is simply to direct our own energy body – including the energy hands which are steered by the energy mind, but also all our other systems – with a healing intention.

That's the job of the conscious mind – to direct attention.

In so doing, the rest follows and does the job it was designed to do in the first place, just as our physical hands and our body get to work automatically when we decide, "I want to go over there and pick that flower."

Our legs start to move, we go there, we bend down, the hands reach out and pick the flower, and all we had to do was to make the original decision, direct attention, and give the command, "Go!"

So you see, energy healing isn't that difficult at all.

By very virtue of our design, and the fact that we have an energy body which contains an energy mind, energy feelers, eyes and ears, and energy hands, energy generators and so forth, we really do have all we need to affect real energy healing – each one of us.

Our conscious minds have an important part to play in that process by holding the focus of attention and directing the actions our bodies (including our energy bodies) are taking; and so in EMO energy healing, body, conscious mind, energy mind, energy body all come together to work on a single outcome - to put to rights what once went wrong; to re-establish the Even Flow, to do real energy healing for the energy body.

Healing The Energy Body In Brief

- Every person has an energy body.

- This energy body has, amongst many other things, hands of energy which can touch, change and heal the energy system because they are of the same material.

- The energy body also has an energy head, which we call the energy mind, which knows how to work with energy, because that is its home dimension.

- It is the job of the conscious mind to direct attention on an erea, to give the instruction to proceed, to hold the focus on the healing attention and encourage the process.

- Over time, we re-learn to trust our healing hands and our energy mind again, but we also begin to understand consciously far more of what is happening, and what they are doing as well.

The Even Flow

Now we nearly have everything we need to affect real energy healing which leads directly to transforming people's emotions.

We have the understanding that all emotions originate in the energy system; and that painful or negative emotions denote that there's something wrong, and happy, positive emotions denote when the energy system is working well.

We have found out that we have healing hands which come free of charge with every person by virtue of design, and an energy mind that understands how the energy system works, and what has to be done.

We have understood that it is the job of the conscious mind to firstly, not get in the way; to secondly, focus and hold attention on the problem erea we are dealing with so that our healing hands and our energy mind can get to work there, and thirdly, to encourage the process as it unfolds.

These things are very simple, and wonderful news indeed; EMO makes working with energy natural, easy, and entirely achievable for the vast majority of people, young and old alike, and regardless of education, economic status, or where they come from in the world.

But there is even better news awaiting us still, and it concerns what we call The Even Flow.

All systems in nature have a place of optimal functioning, where they work as well as they ever can, where they are the very best that they can be.

This state of optimal functioning is what we call The Even Flow.

The EMO concept of Even Flow is not a state of peace, or lying on the ground and doing and feeling nothing, or floating about in out-of-body meditation.

- **The Even Flow is a charged energy state that we humans call being filled with energy, feeling joyful, feeling powerful, feeling "on top of the world," full of life and ready for action.**

A horse that gallops across the grassy field, using its body as it was designed to be used, filled with life and energy is a system in Even Flow, as is a dolphin who streaks through the water, leaping high, in full possession of its physical, mental and energetic capabilities and expressing this in body, mind and spirit.

To work with energy and with EMO correctly, we have to re-learn that the Even Flow is not some quiet, calm or meditative state of "peace" or pain cessation; it is on the other side of that Zero Point Of Peace that so many people strive for, simply because they want to get out of pain.

The Even Flow, the optimal functioning of a system, is on the other side and beyond the Zero Point of Peace and it is not peace a natural system seeks, but its own Even Flow – a fully charged state of activity and energy.

Emotional Pain ➤ Feeling Nothing ➤ Happiness/Even Flow
Negative Emotions ➤ Zero Point of Peace ➤ Positive Emotions

In a nutshell, we are not designed to feel nothing, **but to feel good.**

It is only when we feel good that the Even Flow is established, and we are working as we were designed by the Creative Order in the first place.

And now to the really good news.

- **Every natural system has a natural, inborn drive
  towards the Even Flow, that optimal functioning.**

Systems strive all the time to repair themselves and return to that Even Flow; there is a huge groundswell, a natural lifting pushing all systems and including the human body and the human energy system towards this state of real, energized, active health.

When we work with EMO, we are helped all the time, and every step of the way, by the very fact that the human energy body is designed to restore itself.

There is a template for the human energy body, one for each person, utterly unique to that person that knows what the Even Flow for that one person should be like, and as long as a person is alive, the system will try its utmost to move towards that template of the Even Flow.

In essence and rather than having to "make a healing from nothing" what we are doing in EMO is to assist this natural, inbuilt drive towards real health and optimal function, the drive towards the Even Flow, in every way we can.

We are not doing anything artificial, we are not adding anything artificial – we work with the Creative Order lifting us, helping us, guiding us all the time in the right direction, towards the Even Flow.

I believe that it is because we work with the Creative Order rather than against it that EMO is so beautifully effective.

- **We are not alone in our attempts to restore the Even
  Flow – we have the entire Creative Order and all the
  laws of nature on our side.**

That is truly remarkable, and takes a huge weight of burden off the shoulders when we set about making a real difference and putting to right what once went wrong.

In practice, when we start to work with the energy system for real, what we find is that we start with emotional pain.

As we begin to pay attention to the erea of disturbance, energy begins to flow again through that erea and into the rest of the energy body. As soon as that happens, the emotions change at the same time and in direct response to the changing energy movements in the energy body.

As the energy flow increases and becomes more and more normal, likewise better and better emotions are being experienced.

It is really important to know, understand and remember that "cessation of pain" is not the end result of an EMO treatment – we are seeking and finding The Even Flow instead, what we call the EMO Energized End State, when a person is not "just a bit calmer or has stopped crying" but is in fact, re-energized, filled with love, with joy, present, happy – that is the EMO Energized End State, the Even Flow, and the outcome of working with EMO.

Here are the main points about the concept of the EMO Even Flow once more.

The Even Flow In Brief

- There is an optimal functioning for all natural systems, when a system is in Even Flow.

- Even Flow is not a state of peace, but of positive expression of the full potential in mind, body and spirit.

- We know that we are in Even Flow not when we feel at peace, but when we feel strong, powerfully energizing POSITIVE emotions, such as love, joy, and happiness.

- All natural systems and including the human energy body have a powerful, natural drive towards the Even Flow.

- When we work with EMO, we are lifted, guided and aided by this drive towards the Even Flow.

- We don't have to do it all by ourselves, we are supported by the Creative Order itself when we put our attention on wanting to help a system regain the Even Flow.

The EMO Energized End State

Achieving Even Flow or as we also call it, **The EMO Energized End State**, is the goal and purpose of using EMO.

This one of the most challenging concepts in practice as we have found.

People find it simply extraordinary that you can go from the deepest emotional pain to laughing in delight and quite literally dancing around a room (because it is so difficult to sit or stand still when energy is really rushing through your systems!) in such a short time.

We have become used to the idea that emotional healing takes decades, probably from the experiences of many over the years in talking therapy, or by personal experience of having carried significant emotional pain and it hasn't healed and hasn't changed through time.

In order to really unlock the potential of working directly with the energy body, we need to allow ourselves to be surprised and delighted, time and time again, because it really is true that energy is only energy; that it moves in no time at all; that this is not heavy, or hard work, but easy, quick, and natural.

Experience has shown us over the last decade that people simply forget about the Even Flow and the EMO Energized End State and settle for much less than second best – the cessation of pain, even only to a degree.

For many, to have any movement in their stuck, endless emotional pain at all is the only goal and pain cessation or pain reduction is all they hope for or dream of.

This is completely understandable and very human; yet EMO goes much further than that and can do so much more.

- **Once a person has experienced an EMO Energized End State, a condition where the energy doesn't just run smoothly, it rushes through the energy system and brings the person quite literally back to life, the original problem will never return.**

This is a very important fact to understand about working with EMO and energy in this way – once the EMO Energized End State has happened, this is a healing event which means the problem is actually solved completely, cured, finished, over with, and it won't come back.

If the EMO Energized End State has not been reached, and all we have achieved is a slight cessation of discomfort, or even an absence of any type of feeling (the Zero Point of Peace), the problem is not solved and can come back under stress.

It will then have to be treated again.

If we move on, however, past that point where most people stop because they have achieved what they thought was achievable in the past, based on their past experiences, and continue through that barrier that is the Zero Point Of Peace on and out onto the other side of the scale, that of positive emotions and experiences, there comes a moment where **an event happens in the energy system** and the problem is gone.

The EMO Energized End State is an actual healing event, a truly transformational experience, a moment where everything changed for a person.

40

This makes it extremely precious and valuable; but not rare, nor even difficult.

All we have to do is to remind ourselves over and over again to ask for more, to go further, not to stop too soon, not to settle for second best and to aim for that threshold shift experience that is the EMO Energized End State every time.

Changing Your Mind Made Easy With EMO

One of the extraordinary side effects of doing EMO correctly and arriving at a true EMO Energized End State is that quite literally, "everything" changes as a direct result.

Not only do the person's emotions change to actively positive emotions and good feelings in the body (people often say, for example, "I have never felt anything like this before! I have never felt this before! I didn't even know I could feel like this!") but they also *change their mind.*

Experiencing mind change or cognitive change in an instance is a very important and thoroughly unique aspect of using EMO; there is nothing quite like it.

The person who has experienced the EMO Energized End State will as a direct result, and within moments of that experience, rapidly express all manner of new ideas, different beliefs, values and attitudes, and demonstrate by what they say that they have a whole new understanding of themselves, of the situation, of the old problem, and how things are noticeably different now.

In many cases, the EMO Energized End State unlocks a rush of information that was previously absent or not in conscious awareness; people say that it is exactly like an "enlightenment experience."

The internal representations a person makes change dramatically after the EMO Energized End State experience, as do the thoughts they have, and from there, the decisions they will make for the future as well.

This makes EMO into one of the most powerful mind change tools available today. It also makes instant mind change fully ecological. This means that we don't need to worry that this change is for the better, or what effects it might have on the person's future.

As in EMO, we are only putting to rights what once when wrong, only helping to repair that what once was broken, and whatever changes come to a person when energy flows freely again according to their own creative template, we quite literally cannot go wrong with this, or worry about needing to keep this person in pain for longer so that their ecology doesn't suffer.

The energy healing comes first; and the mind changes are nothing more than a clear indication or a symptom of the energy system functioning better again.

It is fascinating to note that people become more reasonable, more rational, more humane and far, far more logical in their assessments of what happened with their problem, how it affected them, and what to do next.

The more the cleanly the energy system runs, the better a person feels, the happier they are – and the more logical they become. That is astonishingly good news, and to me personally, the re-unification of love and logic, a topic very close to my heart.

Physical Changes And The EMO Energized End State

Finally on the topic of the EMO Energized End State, there are the physical changes that happen automatically to a person who is experiencing this.

People who don't yet know EMO or have not experienced it or seen it with their own eyes often ask, "How do you know if the person has had an EMO Energized End State? How can you be sure?"

The first answer is – just look at them.

As the person nears the EMO Energized End State, their body comes into movement.

They are breathing much more deeply, and they are moving – they can't help themselves, the electric sensations in the hands, back, legs, feet, arms, neck is automatically causing physical movement in return.

If they are "tied to the therapy chair" the person will either ask permission to be allowed to stand up, or just jump up because they cannot sit still any longer.

With most people, seeing them **in movement** is a significant change already to how they were when we started – pale, tense, restricted in their movements, tight all over.

There are further indicators which can be clearly seen as we move towards the EMO Energized End State. One of these is skin colour, and skin tone. People flush, blush, and their faces become more relaxed, wrinkles appear much less sharply defined so they look younger, and there is movement especially around the lips and mouth, and around the eyes.

And then, we have the facial expressions, but also full body expressions of happiness, and joy.

People don't just smile with their lips, they start to smile with their hands too, with their whole body; they might laugh out aloud and

44

start to move with excitement, and may say, "I want to dance, I want to jump with joy!"

As the practitioner (or person who is facilitating this) we too can feel the change in the other person in our bodies.

They become radiant and exciting to be close to, and for the practitioner, being in the presence of the EMO Energized End State of another person is also an experience that activates and enlivens the practitioner's mind, spirit (energy system) and their body in turn.

The Challenge Of The EMO Energized End State

The EMO Energized End State is completely real, and it is absolutely achievable on any topic that has its origin in the energy system.

However, the EMO Energized End State is so very different from any other therapy or healing experience that people might have had in the past, that it becomes a challenge to hold it in mind that it is even possible to get close to that.

It is really difficult to consider that one might have been on this Earth for 40, 50, 60 years or more and there are these experiences that are completely achievable, easy, even – but we've never had them, nor have we ever observed someone else having them.

We naturally ask ourselves, "How can this be?"

"Surely, by now I have experienced everything that can be experienced? There can't possibly be anything more …?"

EMO stoutly says right back, "Yes, there is more, and yes, you can experience this more – more joy, different kinds of happiness and excitement, whole new dimensions of loving and being awed by logic - there is a whole array of feelings you have never had before and didn't even know existed."

That's tough on most people to understand, or believe.

And in a way, the only way to convince anyone of the truth of this is to have them experience their own EMO Energized End States.

Once the experience has occurred for the first time, we don't need to "believe" anything any longer – we actually know. We have learned something new through experience, and that settles any argument on the topic.

All we have to remember is that every person has an energy body, that energy wants to flow, and that when it does, we start to feel good, look good and think logically.

And here is the greatest challenge of the EMO Energized End State.

There are no exceptions to the rule that EMO is not complete until the EMO Energized End State has been reached.

"But surely – you mean apart from cases of bereavement?"

No, there is an extraordinary EMO Energized End State for bereavement pain which I call "the immortal beloved" whereby the person not only no longer feels in pain, or bereaved, but in fact feels **in love** with the deceased, with all the emotions that go with being in love – joy, happiness, walking on air, being grateful, feeling so blessed, feeling so loved and so delighted that you knew this person, had them in your life that you want to dance.

"But surely – not in cases where someone has been raped?"

There are no exceptions – every problem has a corresponding EMO Energized End State, any injury healed in the energy body has a corresponding Even Flow.

What exactly that might be in each specific case we can't know until we have taken that one single individual person through to **their own** EMO Energized End State experience.

Some might talk of freedom, of feeling not just safe but as though they were true masters of their own destiny for the first time in their lives.

Some might say that they have fallen in love with themselves, are in awe of what a resilient, powerful and strong person they truly are. It varies from person to person, it is highly individual, but always, always truly delightful.

"But surely – there can be no EMO Energized End State for someone who was abused as a child?

"That must be totally impossible because it's been too long, too hard, too many symptoms, too many days and nights spent in suffering and torture ..."

47

There is always an EMO Energized End State. People don't just have one injury in their energy system, and the worse their symptoms are, the more we can know already that they have sustained many injuries.

Each specific injury has its own specific EMO Energized End State.

People might talk of shame first – where do you feel this in your body? Show me with your hands.

Take it through to the EMO Energized End State, and this injury is healed and the person is delighted, feels fresh and clean, realises they were never dirty at all, never did anything wrong, and always only did what they had to do to keep alive so that this day of healing might finally be reached. Instead of feeling ashamed of themselves, they are amazed at their ability to survive and never give up, they are proud of themselves.

People might talk of not being able to forgive and being so angry – where do you feel this anger in your body? Show me with your hands? And here again, each location, each pain is the starting point on the journey that terminates – ends! - with the EMO Energized End State. When that has been reached, forgiveness is no longer an issue. When the energy system reaches the Even Flow, love, power and logic rule supreme.

And then, there are other injuries, and we simply take them through to healing, one at a time, in due course.

In a way, the experience and truth of the EMO Energized End State re-defines what we mean by "healing".

The truly "healed" state, the Even Flow restored, is "other than" we thought it was.

It is more, it is better, it is extraordinary, joyful – in and of itself, just one experience of a true EMO Energized End State that is the event absolute and the moment when the real, honest, true healing is taking place, changes lives profoundly.

This is the true heart and power of EMO, our test, our goal, what we work towards – the EMO Energized End State, the true Even Flow that is never only cessation of pain, but in fact, nothing but pure joy.

The EMO Creative Template

As we have noted, every person has a totally unique energy system.

At the moment of conception, a template of their own unique energy system came into being that describes this energy system in Even Flow.

We call this blueprint of the individual energy system: **"The Creative Template**."

When we look at another person with a view to helping them heal energy injuries, disturbances and move them towards the Even Flow, we keep the concept of the Creative Template in mind to help guide us to do the very best that can be done for this one real person as they really are, right here, right now.

In much of human doings, people try to be something that they are not, or they can never be – taller, shorter, and importantly, younger.

It is understandable that people try to turn back the clock to "before the accident" or "before it happened to me" or "a time when I was still happy" or "when I was young and fit."

Trying to make a system work in reverse or reversing any natural system causes nothing but chaos and further suffering – all natural systems flow forward towards the future, they can do no other.

By orientating ourselves not on any perceived "idealised" societal standard of youth, or beauty, or what health "should" look like, but instead looking to the Creative Template of this one individual here in front of us, right here and now, we get a sense of what this person could be like if they were in Even Flow.

Then we can hold the heartfelt intention to move the person towards their very own, very personal Even Flow that is right, correct, age appropriate and achievable for real.

This gives us a role model in personal development and self help that is not just safe, but correct, and perfect in every way, for every one of us at this time, at this age.

When we work with other people, the Creative Template gives us guidance and lets us see beyond the person as they present before us, sad, sick, "broken," so we can move towards perfection for that one person who is with us, right here, right now.

This is an extremely powerful and important aspect of working with EMO, and it teaches us to see people in a very different way.

There are many applications of using the Creative Template of an individual person but one of the most important is to stabilise the one who is working with EMO and give them a clear cut goal towards which they can work.

When we are dealing with human emotions, we are easily overwhelmed by stress and our own emotions, and we might think, "This problem is too big, too old, too huge, this person is too broken, it's too late, there is nothing I can do, I'm not enough to fix this."

But as soon as we step back for a moment and consider the Creative Template instead, the original blue print of that person's energy system, we are literally filled with energy again, with hope, with

51

knowing that there is every merit in at least trying to help that person regain as much of their own Even Flow as they possibly can, and that any movement towards the Creative Template is going to be a job very, very well done indeed.

And please, do remember, that any person, even you, me, and him and her is a natural system, made by the Creative Order, and as such, we all have that powerful, powerful drive towards the Even Flow built right into every aspect of every part of our structures, physical and energetic alike.

We are not doing this alone; in EMO, we are working with the systems, and the Creative Order itself has our back.

The EMO Creative Template In Brief

- Just as every person has a set of genes to define the basis of their physical functioning, each person has a creative template for their energy system.

- This creative template describes how the energy system would be in perfect Even Flow at every age of a person, moving through time.

- By focusing on the creative template, we give attention to right role model for this one individual right here, right now.

- We get an idea of what we are trying to achieve in our healing and energy work.

- By focusing on the creative template, we can stop ourselves getting confused and overwhelmed, or getting side tracked into something that hasn't got anything to do with that one unique, particular person and THEIR energy system, THEIR Even Flow, right here and now.

- The creative template guides us and helps us know what to do in our energy work with EMO.

Modern Energism

There are many more significant differences between the energy body and the physical body than not being able to see the energy system with your eyes alone.

Science, as it stands, does not recognise the existence of an energy system because it cannot be measured with the kinds of measuring devices we have at this time.

However, there are certain things about the energy systems of all things in general, and the human energy body in particular, that are so globally true about natural systems, that we presume that they hold for the energy that makes up and flows through our energy bodies as well.

The first and foremost of these global principles is that of future orientation, forward momentum and universal flow.

EMO Future Orientation

There literally is nothing in nature that does not move forward, or flow forward in some kind of unfoldment, evolution of some kind.

The only time we ever observe "time standing still" and nothing moves at all is when people try to make that happen, for example by keeping a car they bought in pristine condition for 50, 60 years so it looks as though it just came out of the showroom.

But all the time, nature moves forward. Iron rusts, and the paint reacts with the sunlight, with the tiny grating particles in the wind. Rubber and plastic deteriorate, as does fabric, wood and leather and it is a constant battle to try to hold back the tides of time.

Waver in your attention and incessant work for one moment, and "nature will take its course". Whenever things are blocked and "non-flowing" in the physical human body, there is trouble; and we are safe to presume that likewise, energy must flow. When we work with energy flow in EMO, we really do not go any further than to say that "energy must flow, in, through, and out".

When energy flows freely and quickly, we feel energized; when the flow slows down, we start to feel less energized, depressed, deflated; when the energy flow slows down dangerously, we start to feel emotional pain in that erea, and when it stops altogether, the emotional pain becomes so strong, it is now called psychosomatic pain and we may expect for physical illness to follow exactly where the emotional pain was felt before in due course.

Now we may speculate about what kind of disturbance might be present that causes for the normal (fast, energized, healthy, Even Flow) flow of energy to be disrupted to the point that it causes physically felt pain. We may have damage in the energy system, or blockages in major channels; we may have energy going down the wrong channels altogether because something is blocking the natural path; there are all sorts of possibilities as to "why it hurts right here".

In the past, people got side tracked by these many possibilities, none of which can be proven or dis-proven materially; and to work with EMO, we don't actually need to know what kind of disturbance we are dealing with in order to affect the energy system and move it towards its Even Flow.

If you remember, we said that our energy hands do the work, guided by the energy mind, and it is only required for us consciously to pay attention, give the right instruction to proceed and a little encouragement along the way.

In EMO we do this when we consciously focus on the disturbance, on the erea where it is located, remind us that "This is only an energy!" and give the instruction to "Soften and Flow!"

We assist this process with our energy hands, and when we work with others as a practitioner of EMO, have them use their energy hands as well, holding the attention to make it so that energy can once more flow freely. In order for that to happen, a healing is required, and the hands of energy, directed by the energy mind, will do the rest.

Future orientation is a key concept of EMO Energy In Motion. We are not doing any form of psychology here, as we are not focusing on the past. We are asking what you feel right now, right here, instead and deal with what is really here.

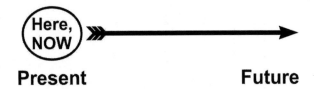

Present   **Future**

EMO is about now, and the future that will unfold from this now. By working this way, we utilise the inbuilt power of the energy system that seeks to move forward in the grand universal procession, to grow (up) and to evolve.

Attention & Energy

I cannot overemphasize just how important our conscious attention is in the greater scheme of things.

Indeed, I would say that as conscious beings, attention is pretty much the only thing we have to make things happen in the energy worlds.

You cannot chop up an energy form with a sword made from iron; you cannot squash an energy form by throwing a boulder on it, and you cannot heal an energetic injury with a surgeon's blade.

In order to affect any energy form,

another energy form is required

In order to affect any energy form, another energy form is required; and we create movements and changes in energy forms automatically when we pay attention and focus on something, want something to happen.

That sounds very easy in theory, and in fact, it is very easy if it wasn't for one thing: namely that people find it really difficult to concentrate their conscious attention on something and keep that concentration there.

This is due to the high stress levels that exist in every modern human being, even in little children already.

Stress de-stabilises mind, body and spirit and causes our focus of attention to become disjointed, jumpy, flashing from here to there, constantly interrupting itself with jumbled up thoughts of this, that and the other.

In order to enter into a process of affecting an erea in the energy body that causes pain, and it doesn't matter if this is in your own energy body or in someone else's if you are assisting in their evolution, we really do need to learn to pay focused attention, and to direct our conscious attention correctly.

In EMO, we are working with one erea at a time; one location that is known because it is felt.

We ask ourselves or the person we are working with, "Where do you feel that in your body? Show me with your hands!"

As the physical hands move to the erea, they give us something to look at, thus engaging our eyes which cannot see the energy system, and keeping the first of our senses interested.

That is really important, as simple as it may seem.

We are absolutely designed and conditioned to "lead with our eyes" as far as attention is concerned. Our attention falls on that which we are looking at, and whatever we are looking at, captures our attention. This also holds true for internal representations, even though we do not see those with the physical eyes in the usual way.

When we try to look at something that cannot be seen with the eyes, such as disturbance in the energy body in a lady's chest who is sitting opposite us, we naturally start to hallucinate and mix up internal representations with the pink jumper and the big silver necklace we can actually see in front of our eyes.

As you can imagine, that is both dangerous as well as really unhelpful; hallucinations are not the way to make a change to something that is really there, in this case, a disturbance in this lady's energy system.

When we ask her to "show us with your hands where it hurts the most," and she puts her hands there, we have something to look at, we can direct our attention naturally, as well as her attention too, because she too can see and feel her own hands.

It is precisely with this simple method that EMO steps out of all the imaginings, fantasy, hallucinations and make believe that has

58

literally bedevilled energy work since the dawn of time and gave it such a bad press.

It really doesn't matter if you are an absolute beginner in energy healing or a 90 year old energy guru who has done nothing but energy work since they were 6 years old; as conscious human beings we need to see the hands showing us where the disturbance is located.

Remember this simple sentence:

"Where do you feel this in your body? Show me with your hands."

It is the breakthrough and beginning of all real energy healing the EMO way.

Now, our attention is in the right place, and for the first time we can say and think the magic words,

"This is only an energy.

And energy needs to flow.

Soften and flow!"

Keeping Attention, Asking Questions

Now, we can pay attention for a short time on this erea, but soon enough, our attention will waver and wander, flash here and there again, and every time it flashes, the process of energy healing is disrupted.

The great challenge is to keep the attention on the unfolding processes in the energy system, and to support these unfolding processes to the best of our abilities.

In order to keep us focused on ourselves, or on another person's unfoldments, we use a simple device which helps us keep paying attention.

We ask questions.

Lots of questions, all through the process.

You can ask these questions of yourself if you are working on healing your own energy body; and I strongly recommend that you ask these questions out aloud, because that engages very different parts of your neurology than if you just try to think these questions to yourself.

When you are working with another person, you need to ask the same questions so you can know what is really going on in that other person's energy system, and you don't have to hallucinate or imagine something is happening which is dangerous and unhelpful.

The most important question we need to keep asking is,

"What is happening? What can you feel?"

The moment we place our healing hands on an erea with a healing intention, there will be something happening to this erea – it will react in some way.

You can tell because your feelings start to change.

Here is an interesting fact about EMO.

60

Small children and people who have never done any personal development, engaged in psychology or self help therapy at all find it a lot easier to tell you how something feels. I guess that we modern highly educated and cerebral folk spent such a long time over-thinking our problems, trying to not feel things, and have practised ignoring our bodies so much, we got very good at it, and now need to re-learn the art of paying attention to subtle changes in sensations in the body.

Luckily, even the act of putting your hands on where it hurts with intention, properly and often for the first time, ever, produces strong feelings; usually these feelings are strong enough to be noticed, and now we are really starting on the process that is EMO.

Energy Flows In, Through & Out

For every possible energy form that we can expect to encounter in our environment, we must have evolved channels to transport this energy in, through, and out.

Even though it may seem that there are certain types of emotions – movements in the energy system – that are so grand, so HUGE, we can't possibly cope with them, there do exist these channels, for all types of energy, all the energy movements and all the emotions a person can expect to encounter in their lifetime.

This is really a question of survival; someone who is "overcome by an emotion" makes easy prey for roaming wolves and lions as they thrash around on the floor, so we can honestly expect that in our long evolutionary history, **storm drains** will have developed to keep us functioning or else we would not even be here today as a species.

The storm drains for the most tremendous floods of emotions do exist; we just need to find them, activate them, take out the blockages and bring back the Even Flow.

When we begin to ask an erea to "soften and flow," the idea is that stuck energy gets directed towards the naturally existing channels and storm drains to carry this type of energy in, through, and out.

So we ask the question, **"Where does this energy need to go?"**

Until and unless you have tried this and experienced EMO properly, you are forgiven to think that you wouldn't know that, but when we do EMO, we only ever deal with a real feeling, a real emotional sensation, that is perfectly real to the person who has it, and they can FEEL it.

They can also feel it respond to the first "Show me with your hands!" physical and attention-energy contact; and they can feel movements when we say, "We want this energy to soften, and flow."

62

An important note: You cannot do EMO "in your head". EMO works with the 6th sense sensations in the body, the real sensations that are emotions. If you do not feel anything, you can't do EMO on it, no more than you can ride a motorcycle if you don't have a motorcycle, or catch a fish in an empty fish tank.

If you are new to EMO and haven't yet experienced how it works, and more importantly, how it feels, you really do need to think of something that would cause you to feel a strong emotion.

The easiest way is to concentrate on something highly positive, sensual or sexual, romantic or otherwise LOVE based.

Take a deep breath, stand up straight and think about something that really excites you, that really turns you on.

Now pay attention to the sensations in your body. What can you feel, and where? What is different now from before you thought about something exciting?

For beginners, re-learning to pay attention to the 6th sense is of the essence, and for the practice of EMO Energy In Motion fundamental.

The pattern is the same, whether we are dealing with negative or positive emotions.

Negative emotions and their sensations change with encouraging energy movement - and so do positive emotions and their sensations.

Now, the person is reporting back their changes.

"I can feel a pressure downwards, I think the energy needs to go down ..."

We encourage those changes strongly by saying, "That's very good," for example, or "Excellent, there is movement!"

We encourage those changes strongly by moving our hands with the movements of the energy. In this example, we follow where the energy needs to flow with our hands, so that the hands are still showing us where there is something going on, and of course, the real healing hands, our hands of energy, are doing further work as keep paying attention to the unfolding events in that person's energy system.

We encourage these changes strongly by re-stating, "This is only an energy. Energy needs to flow. Soften and flow!"

We keep our focus of attention and the healing session on track by asking, "And what is happening now? What can you/I feel now?"

And so a pathway begins to become revealed.

It's the most extraordinary thing, when neither practitioner or client has ever in their lives heard the first thing about where meridians are supposed to be and a clear pathway, a channel becomes revealed, step by step, as the energy flows through the person's body, and they can feel it tingling in their hips, sliding down their legs, finding an exit point in their feet, heels or toes – it is the right channel, not a doubt about it, for this person, for this emotional problem.

The process is so fascinating as these discoveries are being made, as the emotions start to change, as the energy of the person starts to change, that now we don't have to try so hard any more to keep our attention on the unfolding process – it draws us in, becomes absolutely fascinating, and with that comes a deep rapport, with ourselves and our own energy bodies, and with the client when you are working as a practitioner.

Before we go on to find out some truly wonderful things about working in this way with another person, what we call "The Client/Practitioner Dance," here are the main points about the importance of energy and attention in EMO once more in brief.

EMO Energy & Attention In Brief

- Our conscious focus of attention is what starts to bring new movement into old, stuck, disturbed ereas in the energy body.

- If our attention wanders, flashes in and out, is disrupted, the processes of energy healing are disrupted also.

- We keep our attention on the erea in the first place by looking at the hands that show us where the disturbance is located.

- Once the energy starts to move, we keep attention by asking questions about the changes, and where the energy is going.

- We support this process by positive feedback, and by moving the hands and attention along with the movements in the energy body.

- There comes a point when we no longer have to force ourselves to pay attention because we have become fascinated by the process and are in a state of deep rapport with the process itself.

- With practice, our ability to focus attention fluently on energy movements and track them easily as well as support them powerfully, increases and the whole process becomes even easier and more natural still.

The EMO Client/Practitioner Dance

EMO has really nothing to do with standard psychology, talking therapy or counselling. EMO is a modality in its own right, with its own rules of conduct and its own pre-suppositions.

EMO is the first method of the Third Field - modern energism.

As practitioners and users of EMO are not psychologists or doctors, but energists instead, we are dealing with a completely different territory here. This leads naturally to a different way of relating as a practitioner with a client than we were previously used to.

The Client/Practitioner Dance from EMO happened naturally when working with energy in the way we do; it was described after the fact and from the experience of actually doing EMO with a huge variety of people and over many years.

This difference begins at the moment of the first meeting, or when the client and practitioner first come together, and it starts with the practitioner dealing with their own energy system. In short, soften and flow before you even hold out your hand in greeting to the client; as the practitioner, you need to be in a good state of energy flow yourself.

In the past, it was thought that the energy emissions from a client could potentially damage the practitioner and so the practitioners would shield themselves away from the clients, detach, hide behind a clip board, metaphorically speaking.

With EMO we find that if we accept the client and pay attention to their creative template right away, drop shields and soften and flow our own disturbances, a whole new relationship comes into being that is intimate, joyful, and a very positive experience for both client and practitioner, leaving both energized, and delighted they met and had the opportunity to create something quite wonderful between them.

The Energist's Handshake

Developed in the Energist's research lab, we can bring down a true energist's greeting to the following pattern.

Practise this often and with as many people as possible; it gets better and more profound, the more experienced in the ways of EMO you become.

The Energist's Handshake is a three step process we describe as follows.

1. "I don't know who you are."

This is a very powerful statement, something we might say and think to ourselves at the same time, in order to open all our senses to receiving information about this new person.

Someone might "look like Aunty Betty, and she was stupid and annoying," but this new person right here in front of you is not Aunt Betty.

This person is something you have never met before; a wonderfully complex and entirely unique individual, one of a kind, the only one that will ever be in all times spent, all universes travelled.

We don't know who that person is.

To really be confronted with the enormity of this, if we allow it, will cause many sensations, many emotions; as we are letting our shields to this person (which we may have developed against Aunt Betty, but which are entirely irrelevant for this new person here!) dissolve, a lot of energy and information comes into our systems.

Breathe deeply, soften and flow and stabilise yourself; indeed, let the energy rush into you faster and faster until you can sense that uplifting, empowering, which a fast flowing energy system brings to us.

Now, we are ready for the next step. "I don't know who you are ..."

67

2. "But I want to know you."

This is a direct, conscious instruction to all your systems to learn this person.

There is a multitude of information available through our 6 senses; we are used to blocking 90% of it because the conscious mind would get simply overwhelmed.

You can't know a person consciously, ever, but you can make your heartfelt desire known that you would learn as much as you can about them.

"I want to know you," is a decision which once again, may result in powerful emotions which we need to flow in, through and out, and allow the increase jump in information and energy that is being exchanged here to empower us.

We take a deep breath, and here comes the 3rd step in the sequence.

"I don't know who you are, but I want to know you ..."

3. "Show me who you are."

This is another exponential increase in allowing information about this person into your system which is made even more potent by now holding out your hand, taking that other person's hand in yours, laying your second hand upon this and taking a deep breath in as the physical touch heightens the energy exchange.

To be received in this way, without prejudice and a sincere desire to know, learn and understand, is a profound experience for the person in question.

It is possible they have never been greeted in such a way, and it sets the tone for the creation of what I call "the couple bubble" - when two person's energy systems link up, and both become more than their parts in the process.

I don't know who you are.

But I want to know you.

Show me who you are.

Take a deep breath.

Hold out your hand.

Give the energist's greeting:

"Good morning. My name is Silvia, and I am an energist."

The Positive Presence

As a professional energist, is the EMO practitioner's job, purpose and heartfelt desire to help the client find their own Even Flow in accordance to their own creative template, to wholeheartedly assist the client in that and to do the best they can.

This is the same for any energist, at any time, anywhere. We are always seeking to be a positive presence to the people we love, the people we interact with.

There is nothing to fear and so much energy and information to gain.

For energists who work as professional healers and therapists, we can also remember this.

As an EMO practitioner and modern energist, we are not alone.

We have the innate systems that all seek to find the Even Flow on our side, that powerful in built drive towards healing and health which will assist us; but more, we also have the client, the one true expert on the problem, to help us as well.

The "No Hierarchy" Principle In EMO

If you remember, we said earlier that in EMO we do not use maps of the energy body, and instead, work with what is in front of us, right here, right now.

Even the most advanced EMO Master Practitioner in the world doesn't know yet what is going on with another person's unique system, and they have to ask the questions to find out.

The only person who really knows the answers to these questions,

"Where do you feel this in your body?"

"Can you show me with your hands?"

"Where does this energy need to go?"

"What is happening now?"

… is in fact the client.

This places both client and practitioner in a situation where we don't have one helpless, hapless sick person who knows nothing, and one great wondrous powerful guru type who is filled with all the knowledge of the ages and "does all the healing," but instead, we have …

Two equal human beings, no hierarchy,

both working together as a team.

As it takes two to tango, in practitioner assisted EMO energy work you need two to do the healing, and that is not a spiritual idea, or a nice thought, but structural actuality.

The client owns their own energy system, and there is not a thing that will move without their permission haven been given, or without their co-operation.

Change cannot take place in a basic EMO session with a conscious client unless client and practitioner form a couple bubble and start to work together as equal partners in a dance where one responds to the other in real time, having their full attention on what they are trying to achieve together.

Now I use the words "healer" or "practitioner" but that doesn't mean someone who is necessarily a certified EMO Master Practitioner.

Anyone who acts as an energist *is* an energist.

When a mother sees that their child is upset as they come home from school and asks the child, "Where do you feel this upset? Can you show me with your hands?" the mother has become "the practitioner" or "the energist" and the child "the client". If the mother is smart and takes the opportunity to say to the child, "You know, I'm also upset about something. I feel it right here. Will you help me move it?" then the same mother becomes the client, and the child the practitioner.

Further, when that child goes back to school the next day, having learned a neat trick how you can feel better quickly, and their best friend is upset, and the child says, "Where do you feel that upset? Can you show me with your hands?" the child has become the practitioner and the second child is the client now.

And as the second child goes home and finds their mother in hysterics, the second child becomes the practitioner, this other mother becomes the client and so forth.

- **Any time anyone acts as an energist, they are an EMO practitioner in the client/practitioner dance, and the rules are exactly the same for any high ranking paid experienced professional as they are for any person who uses EMO.**

The simple but important rules of basic EMO have some important effects on both the practitioner (as in the sense above) and the client.

The EMO Couple Bubble

The first important effect the structure of the EMO session has is the matter of paying high quality, focused and exclusive attention to the client's energy system.

For the client, attention is all-important. Over the last ten years we have found in the practice of EMO that clients say over and over again, "This is the first time anyone has ever asked me so directly about my emotional pain, I was so grateful that finally someone paid attention to what I was really feeling and gave me a chance to express that."

By paying attention to the real problem erea and asking lots of questions throughout to stay connected with what's happening to the client, the practitioner stays on track and keeps their attention from wandering.

As the mystery of this one particular person's energy system and how they feel the movements of energy in their body unfolds, it becomes more and more interesting to both - this naturally increases attention and that increases rapport between client and practitioner.

They are starting to work together as a team, starting to understand and trust each other, and this is very important in energy work. If we are shielded from each other and disconnected, energy work becomes very difficult if not structurally impossible; so the deep rapport and connection the practitioner and client feel with each other is a wonderful indication that we are doing the right thing.

As the EMO practitioner can also monitor their own feelings and sensations in real time, should they experience a disturbance themselves in response to what the client is feeling, the practitioner can do some self treatment right there and then to keep the connection with the client and the process that absolutely involves both of them.

Keeping The Client Calm & Stress Free

By keeping the focus exclusively on the body sensations, we achieve a significant stress relief in any client right from the start, even if the body sensations are unpleasant in and of themselves. When we give our bodies and minds something to do, a positive action to take that is a step towards solving the problem, we naturally feel we are on the right track and this is stress relieving.

Having someone who is calm and centred and absolutely on your side beside you is also a huge help for the EMO client; the practitioner being stress free by itself and in a good energetic state helps the client feel safe without a word having been spoken.

Next is the notion that "this is only an energy."

It is really difficult to overestimate just how powerfully relaxing that is to say, and to hear the reminder "this is only an energy." This sentence has such a profound effect on a person's mind, body and spirit that the only way I have ever found to explain it is that it is simply the truth, and people recognise that on some level right away, it makes sense, it feels right and that's why it is such a huge relief.

If you ever feel your client becoming stressed or starting to think about other things than the actual sensation of energy moving in their bodies, remind them, "This is only an energy! Soften and flow!" Likewise, do this for your own moments of emotional disturbance. The difference it makes is awesome, simple as it may be.

Then there are some additional de-stressing instructions an EMO practitioner can give to help keep the client balanced.

The first is to remind a person to breathe deeply, in and out. Following this instruction leads to an instant calming of the systems and is highly beneficial to improve energy flow as well. When you are doing EMO by yourself, you also need to be the practitioner as well and so you must remind your self to keep breathing. Say, "Breathe deeply, in and out, that's very good," at any time you notice the client tensing up, locking up, or becoming stressed.

The second easy instruction to help with energy flow and to keep stress levels down is to tell the client to move some part of their body.

We generally encourage the client throughout to touch themselves, massage the erea that hurts, and to use their healing hands of energy to stroke and encourage the energy flow in the direction where the energy needs to go, and that is very stress relieving all by itself.

However, when you pay attention, you can find other body movements to suggest which will help the energy flow. For example, if someone is working on some stuck energy in their throat, and they are all tense and rigid, we can tell them to gently move their neck to encourage the energy flow, or move their shoulders.

It is really interesting to observe how these body movements really help to let the energy flow more freely and as soon as that happens, stress recedes naturally.

Powerful Positive Feedback & Encouragement

EMO clients also say, "I felt so supported all the way through by the practitioner, that really helped me."

One of the most important tasks of the practitioner is to help keep the client focused on the energy movements and the felt sensations by keeping their attention on the feelings in their body; and to encourage the client with strong, positive feedback and heartfelt praise when the client gets it right.

EMO is a mental and physical skill; a new client might never have done anything like this before and they are literally learning on the job, whilst dealing with a big emotional disturbance at the same time.

We learn best when we receive instant positive feedback when we do something right; and in EMO, when you're doing it right, you receive a double positive feedback. Firstly there is the actual sensations as the energy starts to move - "Wow there is something really happening, I can really feel something! This is actually working!" - and in the client/practitioner dance there is also the practitioner's feedback - "That's exactly right, you are doing a good job, you're on the right track, keep doing it, well done!"

Naturally, people can be a little nervous, unsure and scared in this brand new process and for the practitioner to really put their own best energies forward to encourage them, "Yes, that's right, you're doing it right, well done!" is such an important part of the process and the success of the session.

Every little bit of progress, if rewarded in that way right away, gives the client more energy and reduces stress; so when the time comes and you are helping another person with EMO, remember that to praise them strongly and meaningfully is very, very important to the success of the session and to the experience of the client, even if the "client" is your friend, your boss, your superior, your father or your child or a total stranger you found crying on a park bench.

You can and you should give yourself positive feedback when you do EMO in self help as well, when you are the practitioner and the client all rolled into one. Indeed it is my assertion that people who have trouble with doing EMO in self help miss out on this important step, to say to themselves, "I've felt a little movement here, the energy really is moving, that's right, very good, I can do this! Now let's move it more - soften and flow! And remember to keep breathing deeply, and to move! That's good, I'm doing well here ..."

I'd like to add that if you find it difficult to praise yourself or others for doing something right you may have some injuries or blockages in your system; undo those so your "encouraging energy" can help lift you and others to do much better than they could ever do without praise and heartfelt encouragement.

Whole Hearted Healing

The final thing that EMO clients say after their session is, "I felt as though the practitioner really cared."

This last statement is extremely important, because it is so right.

We feel cared for and loved when we are given attention. And we cannot help but respond to this, because attention energy from another person is one of those energy sources that we structurally need for health and happiness.

When a practitioner has shields to the client or starts thinking in their head about all the text books they've read, or about "other cases that might be relevant here" or about their own problems, they are no longer paying attention to the client.

In EMO, that doesn't happen because we are engaged in a fascinating process that is like solving a crime, or unravelling a mystery.

Things happen with the client in real time, right before our very eyes, and if we are the practitioners, we are engaged in the process and we know that we are an important part of the process.

As the client, you feel understood and you can feel the practitioner really wants to help; this makes you like and trust the practitioner more and more as the session unfolds.

This leads to the client and practitioner from both ends moving towards a state of deep rapport we call "the couple bubble", a real connection between them, which is exactly what we need to make this energy interaction work.

You cannot do EMO in your head, and you can't do EMO with another person well until and unless you really are engaged in the process and in a very physical and practical way, really wholeheartedly want this person to re-gain their Even Flow.

The client/practitioner dance is experienced as a wonderful thing for the client who may have never had an experience like that with another person before. It helps and supports the client, keeps them stabilised as the practitioner asks the questions, keeps them calm and stress free, encourages forward movement and gives positive feedback throughout.

For the practitioner, not having to know all the answers and be the only font of healing is a huge relief, a burden released, and this allows the practitioner too to function much better, to be a better healer in fact, and right away.

The client/practitioner dance avoids the practitioner becoming big headed and going on an ego trip, getting a messiah complex, and keeping them firmly rooted in the here and now.

Most of all, however, the practitioner of EMO benefits from that deep connection, the rapport they are in with the client. As the energy starts to move for the client, the EMO practitioner gets to feel that increase in energy through the connection they have with the client, they get to take part in that healing experience in a very personal and direct way.

That is very exciting and rewarding, and leaves the EMO practitioner delighted and just as "high" as the client at the end of a session, not all deflated, sucked dry and all "healed out".

Further, in an EMO session, the client is not the only one who has to do their EMO to get over emotional blockages and painful feelings in their body.

If for whatever reason the practitioner experiences unwanted emotional responses, such as fear, anxiety, doubt they can help the client, or one of their own old "issues" gets touched upon during the session and causes them to flinch, they can do some "softening and flowing" on themselves, right there and then.

This is the true beauty of EMO – you don't have to take time out in therapy for helping yourself flow freely again if something causes you to become unbalanced, or wait for later on to bring this problem to another practitioner.

EMO works best right at the moment when these emotions are experienced, because that is when they are "right there," when you feel them in your body, you know the location, you can say to yourself, "This is only an energy ..." and you can give the command to "Soften and Flow!" right at the moment when it is needed.

That is a huge gift, and makes EMO practitioner/client sessions into an opportunity for the practitioner to not just learn more about energy, to not just have an experience of deep rapport with another person, to not just take part in THEIR healing in a very practical sense, but also each client represents an opportunity to find problem ereas in the practitioner's own systems and heal those too.

- **EMO does not just "heal" the client, but it also evolves the practitioner.**

There is a further side effect from the client/practitioner dance which makes EMO absolutely unique as a healing modality.

As client and practitioner work together to solve the mystery of the problem, and solve the problem, both learn that there is a cause and effect between feelings, thoughts, behaviours and the energy system.

I have mentioned this before, the simple idea that "We are not crazy!" and that there was a good reason for the way we felt, is in many instances, a life saver.

The experience a client has of actually moving energy through the body, that you can feel that, and that it was **you who did that** is quite extraordinary and has big repercussions on a person's self image, on their self esteem, and how they view their own abilities to keep themselves safe in this life.

Starting with a bad emotional pain, and transforming this with nothing but intention and the help of the energy system and the creative order into a whole new experience of feeling alive, feeling happy, feeling joy is a breakthrough in more ways than one.

If we can change the way we feel, then what else is possible?

If we can really heal our old emotional wounds, scars and burdens, then what does that mean for our futures?

If we don't have to be afraid of painful emotions any longer, then what could we go and do we never thought we could?

These are the kinds of things clients will talk about after the energy flow has been restored; these "breakthrough" thoughts people have after an EMO experience come into being exactly because now, there is more energy flow in their systems, they feel more "like themselves" than they've done for a long time (or sometimes, than they've ever felt!), and now, there is hope.

Don't underestimate the enormity of that little four letter word.

Hope is a dawning that comes when not all is perfect yet, but we can really FEEL that there is movement, forward movement, a chance for things to get better.

In all healing, I don't think there is anything more important than hope – both in the client, as well as in the practitioner.

That is a priceless outcome, and we can attest from the evidence of the past ten years that this is truly life changing for people.

In the EMO client/practitioner dance, it is not just the practitioner who ends up with a more expectant, more hopeful, more positive self concept and world view; because the client gave their own contribution from their end, and were materially responsible for the healing, and they know that, the client also gets the benefit of that expansion, of that understanding and that breakthrough that is hope.

Here are the main points once more.

The Client/Practitioner Dance In Brief

–   The "practitioner" is an energist - any person who uses EMO to help another person with their emotional problems, and the conduct is the same for any person as it is for any certified experienced professional.

–   The energist steps up to the client with the intention to help the client find their own Even Flow, guided by the client's Creative Template.

–   The energist uses EMO on themselves so they are happy, strong and looking forward to assist the client in any way they can, to do their very best.

–   As an energist working with EMO, we are not alone. We have the powerful drive of all systems of mind, body and spirit towards the Even Flow on our side, and our most powerful ally is the client themselves.

–   Person and energist work together to find out what is wrong, and how to bring back the Even Flow. This makes them into two equals with no hierarchy (barrier!) between them.

–   By paying focused attention to the person and their problem, and keeping attention on what is right here and now all the time, the energist makes a connection with the client that becomes deeper as the session progresses and that is essential for real energy healing to take place.

–   The energist themselves does their best to stay in Even Flow, to keep their attention on the person's problem erea and to encourage the client throughout. Those the only three important things an EMO practitioner has to worry about.

–   Because of the energetic connections with the person, the energist experiences the evolution too in a personal and powerful way.

– Because they are an equal partner in the healing, the person gains confidence in their own abilities and most importantly, hope.

– Every person is an opportunity for the energist to have a unique energy experience that will evolve the practitioner too.

Healing ONLY The Emotions

So now we have the main building blocks in place which create the basic EMO protocol.

It seems very simple, and on one level, it is, but there are good reasons for each step.

EMO has been extensively tested with thousands of people from all walks of life, and it proves its effectiveness because of that simple structure that works with what there really is, and how people really work.

The EMO protocol is designed based on observation of what people do naturally, and what works. This is a considerable difference between EMO and other approaches, and therefore, EMO does not rely on any leaps of faith and can be tested and tried over and over again with all kinds of human beings, and it will work with the vast majority, predictably and easily.

Firstly, be sure we are dealing with an emotional problem.

EMO works only for the energy system, and is designed to work only with the energy system.

- **EMO is for emotional pain, phantom pain and psychosomatic pain aka pain that has "no physical reason".**

By keeping EMO only for emotional problems, injuries and disturbances, we are keeping EMO clean and clear; plus also, there is no real help for all these kinds of problems available, so by "just" focusing EMO on energy system movements known as emotions we are providing a valuable service that was previously absent.

In a way, by focusing EMO on "emotions only" we are not excluding any kind of problem a person may bring to us, because there is no problem a person might have that does not have an emotional component to it, and when this emotional component has been dealt with, there are often beneficial repercussions across the board.

For example, a person may be dying of a serious illness.

EMO does not promise to cure any form of physical illness, this must be clearly understood.

But there are emotions experienced about the illness and about being ill, about dying, that is something EMO can help a person with.

And please, do not underestimate the value of helping people "only" with their emotions.

People who have been in serious situations and have been helped by EMO to feel better have expressed tremendous gratitude and have spoken often about EMO being a "life saver" - not in the sense that it made the illness go away or extended their physical lives, but in the sense of saving what was left of their lives from being nothing but painful and miserable, and allowing them to have good experiences in their life again, and looking forward to feeling good emotions and even new emotions whilst they are still alive.

- **For EMO to work this kind of magic, we need to keep EMO focused on the emotional aspect of things, and very directly on the feelings in the body, or it will not work properly.**

So in all working with EMO, we need to get to the emotion that is related to the problem first of all, so we have something to work with.

For example, a person may say, "I'm in a terrible state, I am (dying of cancer, nursing my dying husband, have discovered I have AIDS, my business has gone bankrupt, my wife has left me, my child was diagnosed with a lethal illness, I was in a plane crash, I lost my leg, etc.)."

We cannot treat these situations, we can only treat real feelings in the body with EMO, and so the first thing we need to do is to discover the emotion that comes with the problem.

So we might say, "And this is causing you emotional upset?"

Of course, the person will say, "Yes, very much so."

Then we can ask, "Where do you feel this upset the most? Where do you feel it in your body? Can you show me with your hands?"

We might say, "When you think about this, does it upset you? Where do you feel this in your body? Could you show me with your hands?"

It is really important to know that unless you have this physical experience of the emotions, you can't do EMO. Sometimes, people who are not used to actually recognising feelings in their body might say something metaphorical, like, "I feel like drowning in a dark ocean of despair ..." or "I feel like the world has come crashing down around my ears ..." or "It's like I'm trapped and there is no way out ..."

These are metaphorical descriptions and an abstraction of the feeling itself; it is what people do to try and explain to others how they are feeling. In EMO, we need to be much more direct than that, and so we need to keep asking for the actual feeling in the body to start the process, "So this drowning feeling, where do you feel this in your body?" or, "When you think about your world crashing down, how does that make you feel? Where do your feel that in your body?" or, "This trapped feeling with no way out, where do you feel that in your body?"

Remember that you need to find a real physical location first, that is the way out of delusion, or a labyrinth of metaphors and talking and into the reality of the energy system as we experience it. Once we are in that reality, we get to make real changes, and that is why EMO works so effectively, reliably and well.

Talking About Energy

There are many healing approaches which use metaphor and metaphorical representations to talk "about" the problem, sometimes to talk about the energy system.

This can be as simple as talking about auras, nadis, chakras and meridians, all of which are metaphors, and as complicated as talking about one's life in terms of being a landscape that became devastated after a great war and now all the towers have fallen, the fields lie fallow, and starving survivors are roaming the darkened lands.

There is a level in the energy system and the human totality where powerful changes can be made by working with metaphor in that way[1]; but for the workings of EMO, it is of the essence, and I cannot overstate the importance of this, that we do not slip off into metaphor work, but stay with the feelings in the body that really tell us what is going on, and what is happening with energy movements in real time.

So there is a very strict rule in basic EMO that simply states,

"NO METAPHORS!"

I even talk about sending in the metaphor police to come and arrest EMO practitioners who have slipped off into talking about energy in a metaphorical way and are using terms such as "the flowering blossom of your heart chakra" or "imagine there's a great volcano inside of you."

It is the very act of metaphorising the energy system that many of the older forms of energy healing have gone astray, and lost that fine balance between make belief, illusion, fantasy, and the reality of real healing, here and now.

Working with metaphor is subtle, complex, very interesting and indeed. I have spent a lifetime unravelling the complex

---

1   Please see Infinite Creativity, Silvia Hartmann, 2011, DragonRising
    Publishing UK, for advanced energy metaphor work.

interlacements to learn to work with metaphor and energy successfully, but we have to be really clear here and say that **when you work with or think of in terms of metaphor, you are NOT doing real EMO any longer.**

EMO relies on that direct feedback of describing felt sensations in the body as directly as possible, and to keep our attention on simple flow of energy as strictly as possible.

So when someone brings us this metaphor of a devastated land and all its complexities, we say, "Ok, so when you think about that, what is your emotional response? Where do you feel that in your body?"

"I feel a sense of dread."

This is better but it still isn't the place from which we can start to do EMO. We need a physical location associated with the sensation, the feeling in the body. So we ask once more:

"Where do you feel that sense of dread?"

"It's in the pit of my stomach ..."

The minute we take it down to that again, the felt emotion and its location in the body, we are back with something simple and real that we can leverage right away, we can start the easy EMO process by saying, "This is only an energy, it needs to find its rightful channels, soften and flow!" and bring this person relief, then peace, and then an enlightenment event of real change and healing.

At the end of the session, when all EMO has been safely accomplished and the client is vibrantly happy, we can ask them, "Now if you look at that land, what has changed?"

The person will report changes in the metaphor too then, the sun has risen, green grass has grown, the people look happy again and so forth; but the change is **only reflected in the new metaphor**, the change was made at the basic interface where the body meets the energy system, and where we actually feel our emotions.

From Imagination To Sensation

One of the biggest problems with energy work used to be the confusion between imagination and sensation.

As soon as we leave the safety of the really felt body sensations that tell us where and how energy is moving through the body, we step quite literally into quicksand and lose that direct pathway to a resolution that EMO will provide, if it is done correctly.

- **Please do not use the word "imagine."**

If you tell people to "imagine the energy is starting to flow" you will lose a quarter of the population right there because they think they can't make pictures in their minds and their energy system goes on strike. At the same time, those people who can imagine and are good at it will make a mental movement out of the body and into an imaginary intrapersonal world (we call it the Sanctuary) which is no longer directly connected with the experiences in the body, here and now. When that happens, the leverage over the energy system that is so simple and direct in EMO is lost, and with it the effectiveness and power of EMO treatments.

To help make this clear, note the difference between, "I'm imagining being in emotional pain," and "I'm in emotional pain and I feel it in my stomach." Or, "I imagine an energy flowing down my back," and "I can feel an energy flowing down my back."

In EMO, we are dealing with the 6th sense of felt body sensations that have no physical origin, and that is where the conscious attention is directed when we ask people to pay attention to what they sense and what they feel, to their feelings, emotions, and sensations.

For some people who are very good at imagining things, it takes a little while to retrain themselves to think in terms of paying attention to sensations and feelings directly but as I can personally attest, it is worth doing because of the instant increase in effectiveness of treatments and self treatments.

It's Only An Erea ...

This is a good time to remind ourselves that likewise, we try and abstain from using metaphors for the diagnosis of an energy problem.

As we have noted, we don't really know for sure what goes in the energy system, how it really works, and no maps have been drawn of any one person's own personal real energy system.

Likewise, we don't really know when we feel emotional pain whether this pain is caused by some kind of injury or a blockage, or a combination of both; or some other energy form that we don't even know what that might be, or where it has come from.

In the past, people really have gotten themselves into trouble by putting all sorts of metaphors onto energy occurrences, and then forgotten that were dealing only with a metaphor, took the metaphor literally, and now "really think they have a demon attached to their throat who is sucking out their life blood."

You can go crazy thinking such things, easily ...

Or, for example, there was a lady who had been told by a psychic that she had "maggots in her womb" as a result of being sexually abused as a child.

She was so distressed by this, it took quite a bit of calming down and explaining to her that we were only dealing with energy, with an erea of disturbance, and being energy, we could heal this, whatever it might be. The psychic had noticed "something" but they made it much worse for the lady by using the unfortunate metaphorical description for what we would call simply an erea.

As this example shows, metaphors in the wrong places are not just counter-productive to the process of flowing energy and real energy healing, they can be extremely dangerous as in the case above; and as we really do not know what we are dealing with, it is simply safer to re-educate ourselves to think in terms of an erea (existing energetic reality) whenever we are faced with "some thing made from energy that causes a noticeable effect on this person."

Further, as we have said, it is the energy mind and the healing hands of energy that need to do the work, whatever this might entail; and by staying non-specific, we are consciously getting out of the way and allowing those aspects of us that actually know what is happening here, to get to work.

This has the advantage that the moment we stop thinking in terms of "terrible wounds inflicted in childhood," "demons on our shoulders" and "maggots in the womb," "holes in the aura" or "chakras spinning backwards" and start thinking simply, "This is only an energetic reality. We want to bring back the Even Flow. Let's get to work on this erea with a will to heal!" we then …

- Stop being afraid or stressed or confused

- Which significantly helps when you are trying to hold a clean healing intention

- And which makes whatever healing processes need to take place, really simple, structurally sound, clean, and most of all, effective.

The Metaphor Of Water

It is structurally impossible to have a conversation with a client or with ourselves, for that matter, without some form of metaphor, or else we would have no words at all.

If you remember, we move energy with our attention, and what happens is directly linked to how we shape that attention with our thoughts.

So for example, a person might describe a blockage in their chest that causes them great pain as being "Like a big, black rock that presses the life out of me."

We think of the blockage or erea, for that is what it is, an existing energetic reality, in terms of a big black rock, and it becomes a big, heavy problem that we might not have the energy to move.

This directly, and I mean directly, affects the instructions we are giving our healing hands. They may stop, falter, turn off in direct response to such thoughts.

So it is essential for EMO that the practitioner always remembers that we are not dealing with a big, black rock, but that in fact, this is only an energy.

And energy needs to flow, to move.

More, energy wants to move as this is its natural Even Flow. All we have to do is to assist it and it it will flow when we tell it to do so – but only if it is an energy, and not if it is a big black rock.

Therefore, and regardless of what metaphor a client might bring to the table, in EMO we always remind them – and ourselves! - that this is **only an energy**, and that we want it to "soften, and flow".

So that we have something we can conceptualise, consciously understand, and talk about, we think of energy in terms of water.

Water is the only metaphor "allowed" in EMO, and it is flexible and as good a metaphor as we can find at this time to describe the many different states of energy and its flow through our systems.

Water can be so light and fine that it fills all the spaces between heaven and earth and we can't even see it, like on a clear October day.

It can condense into clouds, or a fog or mist; it can fall like rain or spark up like a fountain.

Water can flow freely like the lightest, freshest, sparkliest spring water cascading down a mountain, full of energy, full of life.

It can flow smoothly like a stately river.

Water can become stale and lifeless if it doesn't move, it can become slow and sludgy, thickening like wax as it cools and it can condense down into ice and become hard; and then harder still like old glacial ice, and even harder than that, when all movement stops at 0 Kelvin and all energy flow has ceased.

We can use this metaphor of water to help ourselves and a client understand that we are not dealing with a rock, or a cork, or a concrete dam, or shards of glass stuck in a chakra or such; we say, "This is only an energy, think of it like water that needs to thaw, flow, find its rightful channels, find its rightful path ..."

We can also use this energy and water metaphor to help us understand that all the other many labels we have for emotions are also only metaphors. We are not trying to soften and flow "anger" or "shame" or "depression" - like rock, stone and scissors these are also the wrong metaphor and they don't fit through an energy channel, in a manner of speaking.

In essence, you can't move metaphors with your intention, nor words, concepts, labels, nor even emotions as such – **you can only move energy**.

It is both exquisite as well as extraordinary that as soon as we start to think in terms of energy correctly, energy really starts to move, and you can feel this like you have never felt energy move before.

If you ever find yourself getting stuck in an EMO session, the very first thing to remember is "This is only an energy!"

The minute you do that, your mind focuses itself in the right way; the energy system responds, your healing hands and healing intentions come online, and EMO becomes easy again.

So here are the very important points about thinking about energy once more in brief.

Thinking About Energy In Brief

- In EMO, we direct attention to the 6th sense of felt body sensations that have no physical origin. Instead of imagining anything, we use the words feel and sense instead.

- We cannot move rocks, metaphors, memories, words or even emotions or feelings with our intention – we only move energy.

- Likewise, it really helps to remind ourselves that any form of felt energy manifestation is also "only an erea" - an existing energetic reality, an energy existence, and we can affect energy with our intention, making healing not just easy, but even possible in the first place.

- The only metaphor for energy allowed in EMO is the metaphor of water in its many different states and manifestations.

- When we remember that "This is only an energy!" (and it wants and needs to flow in, through and out, all we have to do is help it on its way) and work with the correct sensory modality of feelings in the body, EMO becomes easy and extremely effective.

Talking About Emotions

The structural way in which EMO works has three huge advantages for client and practitioner alike.

No Need To Label, No Need To Name

The first is that there is no need to talk about emotions.

This means we don't have to be able to put a name to a feeling in the body before we can heal it. We do not have to know if this feeling is called "anger" or "shame" or give it any kind of name at all, which allows us to treat feelings that have no name, and cannot really be described with the usual emotional labels.

From the practitioner's standpoint, by not labelling emotions to be this or that, we don't get confused into thinking that this person's anger is the same as ours, or that of another person who lives down the road, and we can always treat exactly the right occurrence in the right way.

There is also the effect of losing secondary emotions that come about as a result of the labelling process of emotions.

For example, someone who is angry at their father might experience secondary conflicts as they feel guilty about being angry, and then angry about being guilty about being angry, and then upset about feeling angry about feeling guilty about feeling angry and so forth.

By dropping the "angry" label and simply saying, "Where do you feel this feeling in your body when your father says you are no good?" we are also taking out the need for all these secondary convolutions, as we are now simply dealing with a structural injury that once it is healed, will make all discussions on whether it is a sign of being a bad person if one hates one's father totally irrelevant and unnecessary.

There are many concepts related to the way we talk about emotions that become entirely irrelevant and immaterial once we start talking about energy and feelings in this simple structural way.

Concepts such as forgiveness, for example, resolve themselves when we understand that a person cannot "forgive" anything whilst they are still in pain, and that forgiveness is what happens automatically after they have been healed of the problem.

This makes "forgiveness" - true forgiveness, at that! - structurally possible and entirely achievable, and this is how we do it: we simply ask, "Where does it still hurt today?" and heal that. When that is healed, forgiveness has happened as a structural by-the-by.

Take a moment to really allow yourself to contemplate just how revolutionary it is in the treatment of human emotions to not have to label emotions any longer, and to have a method and a **direct** pathway by which we can obtain the opposites of negative emotions so readily and easily.

Simply taking out all the secondary emotions that come about when we think about emotions, and have emotions about emotions, is a huge gift and a huge, huge sigh of relief – and it makes understanding how emotions really work so much easier and more natural, too.

Secret Therapy

The second huge advantage of talking about emotions in this simple and strictly structural way of describing physical feelings and their locations in the body is that neither the practitioner nor even the client need to know anything about the cause of the problem at all and they can still heal it without further ado.

With talking therapies, unless the client "opened up to the practitioner" (and this is a phrase that may well denote what we might call "dropping shields" in energy work!) and told the practitioner exactly what happened and how that made them feel in words, no progress can be made.

EMO works very differently as we are not doing psychology or psychotherapy, but instead, simple energy healing or healing of the energy body.

This working on a "need to know only basis" has multiple advantages, and here are just a few of these.

People can find healing for problems they cannot describe, have no words for, or don't even know themselves what it is. All they have to know is that it hurts, and where it hurts, and healing can proceed immediately. This makes it possible to heal injuries with EMO that may be related to consciously repressed memories, completely forgotten memories or erased memories, as well as pre-verbal memories from earliest childhood or even before birth and regardless of when the injury in the energy system occurred which is causing the pain right here and now.

People can finally find healing who find the idea of talking about that which caused the problem, or even thinking in that direction, simply unbearable and will avoid anything they can to "go there again." They don't need to be afraid of healing any longer – they won't have to talk about their childhoods, or their worst moments and their worst experiences, they don't even have to think about them.

All they have to do is to show the practitioner where it hurts, right now, with their hands, and that is all. I can sincerely say that the relief for many such people to have found EMO was simply immeasurable. Often they were accused, and may even have accused themselves, of "not wanting to be healed" - but nothing could be further from the truth, it was the fear of more pain that kept them away from therapy, and often, quite rightfully so.

People who can't or won't talk about their "emotions" in the old sense of the word, because they have been entrained that it is unacceptable to experience emotions can receive healing now. All they have to do be able to do is to give factual, actual descriptions of conditions in their body, for example to be able to say, "I feel pressure in my chest, and a tightness in my stomach."

This opens up the possibility of seeking healing, and actually receiving healing, to the vast majority of humanity, and including whole cultures and societal sub groups who would never have been able to consider "entering into therapy" as it used to be.

A person doesn't need to tell the EMO practitioner anything at all about the problem to receive help right away.

This is of course immensely important with problems that are perceived as shameful, or self incriminating, "unmentionable," or may even lead to prosecution if they were known to exist.

The fact that the practitioner doesn't need to know what the problem is also allows for treatments of people for whom secrecy or confidentiality is of the essence, as would be the case with famous people, high ranking leaders in industry, politics, civil servants and army and security personnel, and who would not have been able to seek help with emotional problems before.

It is also helpful when working with children who do not have the vocabulary for talking therapy, or anyone who is afraid to reveal the reasons for their problems for whatever reason.

EMO opens the door for all those people who can't or won't talk **about** their problems to find healing nonetheless, and that is truly remarkable and a "unique selling proposition" that if you were to become a professional EMO Master Practitioner, to make sure that all your advertisements include a reference to this feature of not needing to "delve into the causes" of the problem in order to heal the problem.

Communicating About Emotions

The third and final benefit of talking about emotions in the EMO way, namely by replacing word labels and emotional metaphors by simple, structural descriptions of what is felt and where it is felt in the body, we have a whole new way of communicating emotions to other people around us, whether we are doing any healing, or not.

To go through the labels and straight to the feelings is a revolution in communicating with other people and especially your loved ones.

It is commonly held for example that you can't get a teenage boy or the sergeant major husband to talk about their emotions, and many women especially cite how frustrating it is for them that they cannot give or receive the emotional support that is so clearly needed because people reject the talking about emotions/talking therapy approaches.

Conversely, many men get very frustrated because they would love to provide more emotional support to their families, but they have no idea how to do that.

When we stick to factual descriptions of the feelings in our bodies, something amazing happens – other people, including sergeant majors and young children, begin to understand what we are trying to communicate, and they naturally and automatically respond by becoming emotionally supportive and helpful.

One example that I will always remember happened shortly after I first learned about this, lying on the couch, not feeling well, and my then three year old son came into the room and asked for some cookies.

Instead of saying, "I'm poorly, go away," or pretending there was nothing wrong, I told him honestly and precisely about the feelings in my body. I said, "I'm not feeling well. My head hurts, my shoulders are cold and locked up tight, and my back hurts."

He looked at me for a moment with surprise, then he walked away.

101

I thought nothing of it and returned to feeling miserable, hoping it would go away soon – until a few moments later, the three year old child returned with the colourful duvet he had fetched from his own bed. He put it on top of my chest, arranging it so it would cover my shoulders, and said in a very manner-of-fact way, "Mummy get warm. Mummy feel better. I go get cookies."

The warmth of the colourful blanket and the honest attention from the child did make me feel better; I could feel myself relaxing and a little while later, the headache lifted, too.

I had been emotionally supported, energy healed, EMOd in fact, by a three year old little boy who was held to be on the autistic spectrum.

By stating what you feel in your body rather than talking "about" emotions, as though you were giving a status report on your actual physical functioning, the door opens for people to take action to help you.

When we teach other people and including children to express their emotions in that strictly structural way, even a small child can tell you what's wrong and why they are crying – it hurts in my tummy, it hurts in my head, my legs feel wobbly, my hands are cold …

Once we know that, we can take action; and most importantly, we can then stop naming, blaming, shaming, arguing and instead, head straight for putting to rights what went wrong, making us feel better, helping each other to feel better – and that can be as simple as bringing a blanket when mummy says her shoulders feel cold and locked.

Understanding Your Own Emotions

When we start to think about our emotions in terms of feelings that we have in our own body, which have a location, which have a movement, which are real and have a real cause, life does become very different and we start to understand ourselves and our own emotions in a whole new way.

For example, a person may be at a family gathering, and someone says something that causes an instant emotional response, a gut wrenching response.

Somebody who understands EMO is going to react to this entire situation in a whole new way.

Rather than reflexively flaring up and lashing out with words and hurtful energies in turn, then storming off and declaring a holy war on the perpetrator from that moment forth, the person may take themselves away and treat their pain for a time, and until some level of clarity occurs, and flow has been re-established.

As they do this, they will most likely also notice that they had a similar response in the past to similar comments, and will understand that they are dealing not necessarily with an evil relative who hates them and wants to hurt them, but that they are suffering from an injury in their energy system which has been there for a long time already.

Even a beginning of this form of understanding why we react the way we do literally transforms whatever happens next in all reality, but it also transforms the self concept over time.

People who have been suffering from severe emotional pain and pain responses, such as anger outbursts, temper tantrums, emotional meltdowns for a long time have come to the conclusion that they must be "mad, bad, or dangerous" - usually, all of those together.

When we really understand how this works, how these injuries come into being and the effects they have on how we feel, it is virtually impossible to self hate as one once used to do routinely.

Clearly, we are talking about injuries that simply need healing.

Clearly, a person in severe pain would react like that – exactly like that, and there is nothing mad about it whatsoever. Even the most severe forms of emotional reactions are only a cause-and-effect response to conditions and movements in the energy system, and it is very difficult once you know that to continue to berate yourself for having the experiences you have.

We may have thought many times, "There is seriously something wrong with me ..." and that is true, there is something wrong in terms of there being an injury in the energy system, or many injuries that play back on each other, as the case may be.

However, this very different from thinking that one was born wrong, or that one is evil, or broken, or doomed, or beyond help, compassion and rescue.

Understanding the cause-and-effect of one's own feelings and the movements in the energy body brings back rationality, sanity, and even predictability to daily life.

This is in and of itself a huge stress relief that should never be underestimated.

I have heard it said – and exclaimed! - so many times in different words and phrases, but the sentiment is the same, "Are you really telling me that I'm not totally mad and there really is a reason for why I feel the way I do?"

And yes, of course, there is a reason.

In and of itself to know that is a huge step forward, an evolution towards a totally different self concept, and a totally different level of self appreciation and determination to move forward now and find out just what happens when we start to finally heal our worst afflictions.

Over time, as our personal experience with our own emotional states grows, and our knowledge about our own energy system expands, we learn more and more about ourselves – and we find out we are amazing, worthy of healing in every way, and there is so much more out there for every one of us to experience in the Oceans of Energy – and that too, is priceless.

Talking About Emotions In Brief

- In EMO, we do not label emotions of any kind and simply focus on where the sensations are felt in the body. This is a superb short cut, straight through all the talking and secondary emotional loops to the core of the problem which can then be healed as soon as possible.

- We do not need to know what caused the emotions. This allows us to treat problems that are repressed, are "cause unknown" or which a person cannot or won't talk about.

- By not having to talk about the emotions or their causes, healing of emotional pain is now available to many people who are not allowed to, unwilling or incapable of talking about their problems.

- EMO can help groups of people who could not be helped by talking therapy or who were deemed impossible to help, or resistant to healing, by the old approaches.

- The structural way of describing emotions from EMO allows a totally different way of communicating about emotions, in such a way that other people – including small children – can understand how a person really feels, and can take action to help alleviate the pain that is present here and now.

- By applying the principles of talking about emotions to the way we THINK about our own emotions and feelings, a whole new understanding of the self develops, and the self concept starts to change dramatically for the better as well.

An Example EMO Session

Now let us put all that we have learned about EMO so far together and look at a simple sample EMO session.

This is very typical of what happens in an EMO session.

EMO is in one way, very predictable.

There is a pathway from, "What is your problem?" all the way through the EMO Energized End State where the person laughs when you remind them of the problem.

On the other hand, every single EMO session is unique to that one person and that one practitioner, exciting and new as both client and practitioner together explore the client's energy system and get more Even Flow into it. This causes all manner of changes in mind, body and emotions and that is always exciting and wonderful to be experiencing from the client's vantage point, but also from the practitioner's point of view as they partake in the joy of the client because they are in rapport with their client.

So here we have a client or a person, P for short and an EMO enabled person, an energist for short.

Pay particular attention to:

- How the energist: keeps the focus on the body sensations and keeps asking questions;
- How the energist: keeps using the simple basic EMO phrases to help with the energy flow;
- How the energist: encourages P to use their own healing hands of energy to help the process;
- How the energist: encourages P with positive feedback and strong, heartfelt praise;
- How and when the energist: uses movement and breathing to expedite the energy flow.

107

Energist: "What is the problem? How can I help today?"

P: "I've been terribly stressed at work. This is been going on for a long time now but I'm really worried I am going to have a heart attack. I had some bad turns and my doctor says I'm having panic attacks."

Energist: "I can see this is upsetting you."

P: "Yes, yes it is."

Energist: "Where do you feel that upset in your body? Can you show me with your hands?"

P's hands immediately go to the top of the chest and make circular movements whilst P thinks about it. P looks down at his own hands and says, "I guess it's around here."

Energist: "How does that feel?"

P: "Pressure, swirling, uncomfortable, it interferes with my breathing, I can't breathe right."

Energist: "This is where there is a disturbance in your energy body, there is energy swirling around that is stuck or trapped. It needs to flow away, then you can breathe better."

P nods. P's hands are still on the top of his chest, making small circular massaging movements.

Energist: "Now you have your hands there already, that's really good, it's natural and the right thing to do."

P looks down at his hands and nods.

Energist: "You keep massaging that erea with your hands, and pay attention from the inside, and I am going to help from the outside, and we'll make this flow away.

"Ok, so where does this energy need to go?"

P: "I'm not sure."

Energist: "There is usually the most pressure in the direction where the energy wants to go, wants to flow out, what do you feel, up or down?"

P: "Yeah, yes, it feels as though it wants to go down my arms but is stuck in my shoulders, it can't get down my arms."

Energist: "Yes, that's very good. Can you move your hands and encourage that flow towards the shoulders and down your arms? It is only an energy, we can tell it to soften and flow."

P crosses his arms, starts to stroke his own shoulders with his hands.

Energist: "What's happening?"

P, stroking his shoulders, "I can feel it in my shoulders, its starting to move a bit."

Energist: "Very good! Keep saying to it, soften and flow. It's only an energy and it wants to flow."

P: "Yes, I can feel that. I can feel something moving down my arms. Oh! That feels strange!"

Energist: "That's excellent, that's exactly right. Keep helping it along with your hands, and if you moved a bit, move your neck and shoulders, that really helps to make the energy flow."

P flexes and moves shoulders, moves neck from side to side, strokes now upper arms down to the elbow. "Yes, I can actually feel this. It is really coming down my arms!"

Energist: "Yes, I can feel that too now, it's electric, keep it up, you're doing really well. Soften and flow."

P now stroking lower arms, and all across towards the top of the hand and fingers, left hand first.

Energist: "Tell me what's happening."

P: "It's coming out of my fingertips, I can actually feel my hands tingling, actually my whole arm is tingling, and all the way up to my neck!"

Energist: "That's so good! You are doing so well! Now breathe deeply, and let that energy flow out of your hands."

P, stroking lower arms and hands, moving his hands, shaking them out, still moving shoulders, neck and spine as well, looking excited, starting to smile.

Energist: "What are you feeling?"

P, smiling, "I don't know – it's really hard to describe. Like electricity flowing down my arms and out of my hands. It feels – unusual, nice, I like it!"

Energist: "Ok, so turn your attention back on your chest, where it started. Think about the pressure at work and the feelings of overwhelm, about the heart attack, what does that feel like now?"

P rubs hands over top of the chest and strokes down shoulders and arms, "Much freer, much more open, I can breathe! I can actually breathe!" P smiles and breathes deeply.

Energist: "Do you want to stand up for a moment?"

P: "Yes please, I'd like that."

P stands up and moves and flexes all over, shoulder blades really moving up and down now, moving from the hips, moving his hands and arms, "I can't believe how much better this feels, how much better I feel! Everything looks brighter. I feel – alive, how weird is that!"

Energist: laughs. "That's EMO."

P: "So this was really only an energy? Amazing ..."

For this person, on this occasion, there was a problem with an energy flow that came up the centre of the body, then split into two paths that went close to the top of the shoulders, and there it was blocked, causing the energy to circulate round and round, rather than to flow.

This in turn caused difficulties with breathing and the more energy got stuck there, the more frightening and painful the physical sensations became, until P experienced what was called an anxiety attack.

The energy needed to go down his arms and out of his fingers, and the pressure on and in the chest went away, P could breathe again, and also think clearly again.

As this was a primary place of blockage for P, he was reminded when the feelings in the chest came back, to self treat as he had done in the session to encourage the energy flow.

All this is extremely simple, logical, and for P, proof that he has energy system, that he can feel it, and most importantly, that he can improve his own energy flow by encouraging energy flow in his own particular "trouble spots" or fault lines, as we call them, by himself, and when it is needed, right there, and then.

A few things I'd like to point out about this fairly typical EMO session.

If you read through it afresh, notice:

How the energist: keeps asking what's going on, to stay involved in the process, and it is P who leads with his own feelings and what is happening to him at the time.

That the energist: keeps encouraging P all the way through, and this is really important. P might be worried whether he's doing this right, and it is new to P, so the encouragement really helps P to stay focused on encouraging the energy flow.

the energist: also encourages P to **move**, and to **breathe**. Those two things are profoundly simple, but they really impact the energy flow tremendously; this is also important to remember when you are doing EMO by yourself. When we start to concentrate, we often automatically lock up, stop moving, stop breathing, and loosening up with movement relaxes and unlocks the whole system.

Also, and this is a very important feature we have discovered about doing EMO, the person's own body often knows what to do to help the energy flow along. **If the body is allowed to move any way it wants to, it creates movements that are particularly designed to improve energy flow** – and there, we are engaging the body's own "wisdom" as well as the body's desire to heal.

Energy needs to move, and body movements are the perfect way to encourage that energy movement. See also Energy Dancing in the Exercises Section for more on this remarkable topic.

In the session with P, you might have noticed that there was very little talking about the problem, or about EMO, for that matter.

This is also important. Talking doesn't get energy to move by itself; and the sooner we get straight down to the real, felt body sensation and start the process of finding out where that energy needs to go, and then to help it go there, the better!

This is not just about saving time, although time is precious, and it's important to get movement into stuck systems as quickly as we can.

Energy needs to move. The person needs to move to encourage energy flow.

And likewise, an EMO session needs to move and not get stuck.

All we need is a problem, a location and then we need to move forward towards the Even Flow.

We don't want to get bogged down in the EMO session, and if you think in terms of the session overall as also having an Even Flow, a perfect progression from the problem to the EMO Energized End

State where the **opposite** of the problem has come into being (which is so much better than "just" having solved the problem!), you can also start to notice when the session itself gets stuck.

By coming back and back to the **actual felt experience** we return to the Even Flow of the session, and that's the same with a client as a practitioner, or as someone who is using EMO in self help.

As soon as you start thinking **about** the problem, rather than **feeling** the problem, you can lose the flow of the session; and the simple remedy is to return to the feeling and keep asking yourself or your client, "What's happening in your body? What can you feel? And where do you feel that?"

People Who Can't Or Won't Do EMO

EMO is a simple, practical method for working with the energy body.

EMO works for the vast majority of people, from young children to old people, from all different societies, races and backgrounds, and they don't have to know anything, or be educated in anything at all.

However, for EMO to work a person must want to do EMO, and they must be able to feel emotions in their body.

There are some people who reject the idea of us having energy bodies in the first place; or the idea of emotions being movements of energy conflicts with their belief systems so much that they won't even try to do EMO.

There are also some people, a tiny minority to be sure, who cannot feel energy movements in their body at all. Most of these are on the autistic spectrum and some suffer from some form of medical or psychological condition which precludes the ability to feel emotion.

We have a simple solution for this, which is to say, "Don't do EMO with people who won't or can't do EMO."

There are a million techniques and approaches, often modelled on the few "special cases" amongst the wide variety of human conditions which can be used instead.

- **There is no need to force EMO on anyone, or to fight with a client who won't or can't do EMO.**

Simply do something else instead.

EMO is strictly designed for people who can feel emotion and who want to change the way they feel, or who want to improve conditions in their energy body so they can feel better, think better, and act better as a result.

This is the overwhelming majority of the population on Planet Earth, and it is in essence, normal people that EMO was designed for.

By focusing our attention and effort on those we can help, as opposed to those we cannot help with EMO, we get to help many, many people indeed and do a lot of good in the world.

There is no one single method which can help everyone, although many methods proclaim that they do. EMO works with people who feel emotions and want to work with that.

This is simple, straightforward, and well worth remembering:

Don't try and do EMO with people who can't or won't do EMO.

Do something else instead.

Conclusion To Part I

In this first part, we have learned the basic principles of EMO.

We have talked about emotions being the physical experience of movements in the energy body; that everyone has an energy body, and that this energy body has a head – the energy mind – and of course, it has hands of energy which are custom made to heal the energy body as well.

We have learned a simple method of working with the reality of felt emotions without the need for labelling or talking **about** these emotions, and what the benefits of this direct and simple approach are for both practitioner as well as the client.

We have noted that when we start to think in terms of emotions as energy movements, we also get a new perspective on our own emotions, and the thoughts and actions that have come as result of those emotions.

We have further found out that negative emotions or emotional pain comes directly from a malfunction in the energy system – an injury or a blockage that stops energy from flowing freely.

We have discovered the EMO Energized End State, which is the **opposite** of the problem, not just peace or a cessation of feelings. That's one of the most exciting discoveries from EMO for me personally and it unlocks a whole new world of good and enlivening experiences that many of us never even knew were possible.

We have talked about sensing for the Creative Template can steer us in the right direction, towards the Even Flow for this one particular person, whoever they may be, and of course, our own selves included.

We have found out how important it is to pay attention, and how we pay attention in the client/practitioner dance, where both people are equals and work together with the true desire to restore the Even Flow, to put to rights what once went wrong.

Most of all, we have found evidence that people's emotions are valid, that there are good reasons for them, that it is important to have emotions so we can know where something is wrong in our energy bodies and we go ahead and finally heal that.

For me, the most wonderful discovery of all is that we don't need to be afraid of our own emotions or those of other people, ever again.

All emotions are truly and really, ONLY AN ENERGY.

Once we lose our fear of emotions, and we have a way to treat emotions right there and then, when they occur, in the field, as the saying goes, a whole new world of possibilities becomes revealed, and we find ourselves amazingly, right amidst the Oceans of Energy that were there all along, but we hadn't realised that.

Beyond healing, and sometimes even before healing, there are more amazing wonders to be discovered about the energy dimensions and our own energy body which lives in those energy dimension, which are real, and all around us.

And this brings us to the next important topic of EMO, which is **Energy Nutrition.**

PART 2 – EMO ENERGY NUTRITION

Understanding Energy Nutrition

It is true that before the daily practice of EMO and the direct tie in with the felt sensations of emotions, the whole energy body idea and concept was somewhat at arm's length for most people.

We believed in having energy bodies, sure. We may have undertaken energy drills or engaged with systems and techniques, and we may have made many maps of all manner of occurrences within the ever flowing, ever moving and ever evolving energy body, but still, until the emotions came into it, energy really wasn't that personal.

Something interesting happened after the first few month of feeling the worlds of energy and being consciously aware of that through EMO practice had passed.

We started to talk about the energy body no longer in theoretical terms, or in highly abstracted metaphors, but in a very straightforward way, in the same way we would talk amongst ourselves about our physical bodies.

We started to talk about the head of the energy body which had a mind of its own, the energy mind, and that made a lot of sense at last and alleviated so much confusion when compared with the wild ideas we had about an "unconscious" or "subconscious" before.

We started to talk about how the previously so mysterious "healing hands" were of course, simply the hands of the energy body, and how obvious that was now, and how easy that made it for us to actually really switch on our healing hands of energy, simply by shifting attention and giving the order for it to be done.

And so we also started to talk about the energy body and what its nutritional needs might be; what the energy body eats and drinks, what it needs to survive, and then, what else it needs to really thrive and grow strong, to become really happy.

Were there energy forms that acted like vitamins on the energy body?

Did the energy body have its very own auto-immune system, and how could we set about strengthening and helping that to function better?

What kind of energy diets were people on, and how could we improve that?

The very first energy nutrition insight that really leapt out to me was that of people energies.

Human beings are social mammals, and 98% of our DNA is the same as that of chimpanzees.

There are veritable mountains of research papers that state without a shadow of a doubt that when you remove a social mammal from the group, isolate it in some way, truly terrifying results on the physical and mental health come into being.

Further, all the most disturbing and extreme observed behaviours in social mammals, including attention seeking behaviour disorders, autism, self mutilation, repetitive behaviour disorders, trance behaviours, rage syndrome, and even autism and withdrawals leading to death come into being when an individual is isolated from the group.

There was no real explanation as to why this should be the case – and without taking the reality of the existence of energy, and energy systems and energy exchanges into consideration, indeed, this strange behaviour that is shared by all social mammals and including humans, makes no sense at all.

Mammals are designed to make relationships – connections with others of their own species through which energy flows.

This energy exchange between social mammals is essential to their health and well being and forms the very corner stone of energy nutrition for people.

In the absence of others of their kind, social mammals get so "desperate" - read, desperately **hungry** for those energy flows – that they will cross species boundaries and make relationships with others who are not from their own species.

This is observable everywhere in the animal kingdom, from lonely horses who will make friends with sheep, goats, and cows; lonely dogs who will make friends with cats, rats and rabbits; and there is even a fully documented report on a single wild lioness who tried to make relationships with a human camera crew and with a group of jackals.

We don't have to go far to observe how people do this too.

The lonely lady with the dozens of cats is the tip of an iceberg where people make relationships with animals, and draw energy through those relationships.

But that isn't all there is to energy nutrition.

We cannot just eat all the time, we also need to eliminate.

Energy exchanges between the members of groups of social mammals is a give and take, it is a flow of both drawing in life giving energy, as well as being able to releasing energy that is being generated in the system and that is "taken away" by other members of the group.

- **In EMO energy nutrition, it is just as important to release/disperse/discharge energy flows as it is to draw in energy flows for the energy body to remain healthy.**

Many people think they don't have enough energy and need to "suck in" more energy when in fact their symptoms are in place because they cannot discharge enough energy for a healthy flow in -> through -> and out of the energy body to come into being.

Energy nutrition – the entire digestive system of the energy body – has to be through flow of energies, a fast flowing river of all manner of energy forms and flows which are needed to keep the energy body healthy.

In other words, we do not only need to give love and attention to others, but we also need to be able to take it from them in turn; and it is exactly there where we first met up with the shields.

Shields

When we first started to research EMO and try out many different things, one might say we played with EMO just like you would with any exciting, shiny new toy, we played The Insults Game.

This is a great exercise in EMO, as we take a special phrase that has meaning for one particular person and "throw it at them" - causing the physical pain response that tells us where the energy injury is situated in the energy body.

For example, a person who was told that "You are a total loser!" by their father and these words are highly meaningful and painful to them, would instruct a second person to shout those exact words at them.

When the helper or practitioner got the tone of voice right, the person would experience the same painful emotion in the same location where they experienced their father's voice in the first place; and then energy healing would commence, according to the simple EMO procedure of finding the right channels for this incoming energy form, softening and flowing, and tracing a path in, through and out the energy system.

Then the insult would be repeated, and the speed of the flow of energy in, through and out increased until there was a threshold shift and the EMO Energized End State comes into being.

The result of this is that the person starts to laugh when the helper shouts the old insult at them – and has many very interesting, helpful and correct cognitive insights and ideas, and experiences an increase in compassion and love for their father as well.

The Insults Game is a great convincer and practice piece.

But there is another part to the Insults Game, and that is the Praise Game.

Here, the person is told something different.

125

They are told, "You are beautiful," for example.

And what happens?

Instead of embracing this incoming energy, "sucking it in" and starting to glow with joy whilst exclaiming, "Thank you so much, I've waited my whole life to hear this!" people just stand, motionless, sad, untouched. They might sigh, raise an eyebrow, shrug their shoulders. They say, "I don't feel anything ..."

The energy form isn't coming in.

Something is stopping the energy form from "touching them" - literally, touching the energy body so that it causes a real felt sensation or emotion.

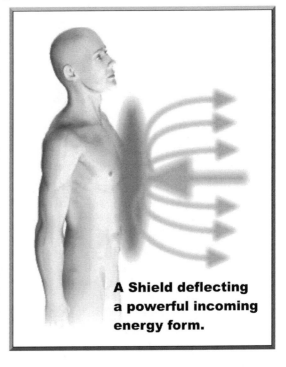

This was were we learned about the phenomena of "shields" - very specific energy forms designed to keep very specific energy flows from coming into the energy body.

So we ask, "What is happening to that incoming energy? Can you show me with your hands where it is blocked, where the shield is?"

A Shield deflecting a powerful incoming energy form.

Amazingly, people's hands will move automatically and show the shape and size of the shield, and the location.

Once you start looking for shields, and the way people's hands and body movements show these for all to see, you will be able to notice shields everywhere.

126

They are absolutely real, they really do exist, and they cause havoc in the flow of energy nutrition, which is so essential for a healthy energy body.

These shields also have tremendous side effects on a person's experience of life, and the meanings they make, the thoughts they have about themselves and others, which in turn causes secondary emotions and all manner of destructive behaviours.

For example, a very beautiful woman who is a model and is being told by everyone that she is the most beautiful woman on Earth today, may never experience the reality of this because of a shield.

As far as she is concerned, not only are all these other people lying and/or totally deluded, which now causes further breakdowns in all of her relationships, she still hungers **desperately** for that exact energy form, approval, admiration, attention and love which even if it is given, she cannot receive.

And yet, there are all those magazines with her face and body on them; her reality doesn't make sense, her life doesn't make sense, the hunger doesn't go away, and this beautiful woman might descend into self destruction, self medication, addictions, and all manner of disturbed behaviours which **also** don't make sense to anyone at all as she is clearly, beautiful, rich, and beloved by all.

One shield – an entire incarnation in ruin.

Shields are that powerful; they are that important, and when you really start to understand shields and how they work in your own life and that of others, many, **many** previously inexplicable aspects of human behaviour start to make perfect sense.

Better than that, with EMO you can start to change things dramatically.

- **Shields are made from energy, and that means they are ONLY ENERGY.**

Shields and the energy forms that they are made from underlie all the general rules of the energy universe and they can be manipulated, moved, and changed with intention energy.

Even though shields can have such enormous repercussions and spawn a multitude of the most extreme mental, emotional and physical disturbances, the shields themselves are simply energy and very easy to deal with – if you follow some basic safety procedures.

Where Do Shields Come From?

The first time we ever simply removed a shield to an incoming positive energy form, such as, "You are beautiful," the person in question cried out in pain, wrapped their arms around their chest and dropped to their knees, then curled up in the foetal position on the floor, as though they had been shot with a hard bullet in real time.

And there it became clear why people have shields, and why they come into being – a shield is there to protect an existing energetic injury.

A shield is like the energy body version of a scab, or a plaster, if you will.

It protects that which lies behind the shield so it is not further damaged by further incoming energies in that erea, which the erea cannot process because it is damaged and needs to be healed.

A shield is most likely not something that a person made in consciousness to protect themselves from further damage, but simply an automatic response from the energy body to having sustained an injury.

This is an important aspect of shields and understanding how they work in people (and in other social mammals!) - the creature in question doesn't "choose" to make shields to love and admiration, to help and healing, to moral support and offers of kindness and attention.

The shields grow automatically when the person or creature has been injured.

It is not their fault that they can't "accept our love, healing and assistance".

They are not "rejecting us" because they want to suffer, or they hate us.

They simply have a shield and beneath that shield, there lies the original injury which is crying out for healing.

Once you know this, the path to healing becomes easy.

When we do EMO with people who have shields, we now no longer dream of simply taking the shield away; we now know better than that.

We appreciate the need for the shield and its protective function; and we absolutely hold that the only person who should ever do anything with the shield at all is the person to whom it belongs.

If we are assisting another person in the removal of a shield, we may suggest certain things, but we never, ever do anything from our end other than to support the person whose shield, whose energetic injury, and whose pain we are dealing with.

How To Remove A Shield

The first step to removing a shield is to discover the energetic injury behind the shield.

Instead of taking it down altogether, we want to let just a tiny bit of the energy flow which is causing the shield to be there through and into the energy body.

We say, "Make a tiny hole into the shield, like a pin prick made by the finest laser, and I'm going to send this energy form again. Pay attention to your feelings when I say this again, "You are beautiful."

The beautiful model from our earlier example who thinks, feels **and knows** that she is actually hideously ugly, may nod at this point and then she puts both hands flat on her chest, just above the line of her nipples.

Further Blockage

Main Erea Of Injury

Finding Energetic Injuries by making a pinprick hole into a shield.

She says, "It burns here, all across here, it is really painful."

Now we have the location of the injury, and we can now proceed with normal, simple EMO as before.

We say, "This is an energy disturbance. I help with my attention from the outside, and you pay attention from the inside, let us send some healing energy into that erea.

"Keep your own healing hands of energy on that erea as well and let healing flow into that place that hurts, that burns.

"Where does this energy need to go?"

The model says after a few moments, her hands having made small automatic movements over the era on her chest, "It feels like it wants to go upwards but it can't find the way."

"Let's soften it some more, encourage it to heal, to flow. This is only energy ..."

A little while later, "Yes, I can feel it now. It's like it's gathering in the middle, and from there it can go up ..."

A path was found that left straight through the top of her head, and now the next step in shield removal happens – we ask her to make the microscopic hole in the shield a little bit bigger to let more of that energy in, while the practitioner or helper says again, "You are beautiful."

There may be more healing work to do; but step by step, more and more energy can flow into the erea and be safely transported up, through and out.

Eventually, there comes the moment when the shield disappears entirely; or the person whose shield it is says, "I want the shield to be gone completely."

This is a natural indication that the erea has been healed.

Shields & Personal Evolution

How exactly a shield appears, where it appears, how thick it is, how it is described by a person, and how we go about removing these in sync with healing the energetic injury that lies behind them, varies from person to person.

This is a delightful feature of EMO.

You have a basic structure only, but beyond that, you and your client, friend or loved one are explorers together to find out what to do as you go along.

An experienced EMO trainer once offered to write a list of all the different ways they had found out to remove shields by working with many different people, but I said, "That's very kind but do you want to take away the joy and excitement of discovery that happens every time a practitioner and a person work it out by themselves?"

We really should never allow ourselves to even think about something else or someone else when we do EMO with that one person there, right in front of us.

Allow yourself, no matter how experienced you become in time, to always go on that journey of exploration with the person right there in front of you.

Ask them how they would like to make a small hole in the shield. They might have a different idea, something that is personal to them, just right for them, and that of course, is the perfect method, and the only possible perfect method for that person.

Some people might not want to touch their shields at all.

That is their right and prerogative – it is their energy body, their shield, their injuries.

We might ask them if they want to do something else first, something that needs to be done before we can deal with this shield, this injury it protects.

We should always remind them, however, that we are dealing with energy – this is only an energy.

It is very sad that people have lived in extreme disturbance and pain, and that these untreated injuries and disturbances in their energy systems have caused such grief and trouble over the times of their life, and to so many, and in so many different ways.

It is shocking that with a session which may only last half an hour or so we can so simply deal with something that caused so much pain.

But we always need to remember, and remind ourselves and our clients, friends and family that the past is the past, and the future is where we need to concern ourselves with; and that future arises from the present, and in this present, we simply get to work and heal, repair that what once was broken, because that is the right thing to do.

The relief and joy that comes when the pain is gone, the huge, **huge** benefits we gain in feeling better about ourselves, about our lives, about everything in this world, and the immense increase in love, faith and trust we experience makes it worthwhile to take the leap of faith, to lay down all the suffering of the past, and move forward.

With some people, it might take a little time before they are ready to go forward as fast as EMO will allow – and that is very fast.

Energy work is essentially, instantaneous; or it would be, if we could allow that to be so.

When your client or you yourself become hesitant about healing themselves, about repairing their energy systems and their injuries, improving their entire energy body by the increased energy nutrition that is now coming into all their systems, remind yourself that we are only doing what's right and proper, and should have been done a long time ago already.

The energy system has been waiting for us to take action.

It has sent a million messages calling for help, in feelings, in thoughts, in dreams, in behaviours.

We just didn't understand these messages properly, and now we do – so let us answer them as swiftly, as quickly and as elegantly as possible.

There is no merit in waiting when a person is brought into the ER with a knife sticking out of their chests; and there is no merit in waiting before we heal someone, including ourselves, of an old energetic injury.

The sooner you can get the healing done, the less pain that person has to experience; so by all means, do the best you can to move people as fast as possible past all the worrying about the past and what something might mean they have no conception of as yet; move towards the Even Flow with volition, and with delight.

An Example EMO Session Involving A Shield

Here, we have a lecturer (person P) who feels disconnected from his students and dissatisfied with his profession.

P: "I feel there is something between me and my students when I teach – it is like I can't get through and I can't reach them." (As he talks, he gestures and paints a square block in the air, on a level of his eyes, about a hand span in width in front of his face.)

This might be a good moment to point out that all energy manifestations in EMO can be viewed and tracked by watching a person's physical movements and especially their eye movements, body movements and hand gestures.

Hands especially go to the places that hurt when you ask, long before a person has worked out consciously where something hurts. Hands will also gesture the direction the energy needs to take at the same time as a person will say, "I don't know where it needs to go ..."

Hands paint walls, shields, blockages and all sorts of other existing energetic realities into the room. Hands and eyes point to and look at energy manifestations as a person speaks about their problems so you can know where they are.

Looking carefully at your own gestures and those of other people will show you time and time again where their ghosts are, where their shields are, what they duck away from, what is distasteful to them, what they try to ward off, wave away, motion towards themselves, break through – it is absolutely fascinating.

If you know that these movements and gestures are being directly caused by an energetic occurrence, you can begin to really see a person's private world and limitations; you can see where things are tense, problematic or where it hurts in their bodies and in their wider energy bodies too.

These body movements are never random; they are the physical manifestation of something that is really there, even if it is invisible to the naked eye.

Now, back to our gentleman who had a two foot high and three foot wide block, the width of a hand span, two hand spans out right in front of his eyes which stopped him from contacting and reaching his students. This energetic occurrence is completely defined in time and space by his hand gestures, with co-ordinates and cause and effect of its own existence; he is not imagining it. This is an erea, an existing energetic reality, and it is really there. Let's find out what happens next.

Energist: "That's like a wall of energy. Hm. What would happen if you kind of looked over that for a moment?"

P (cranes neck in response and withdraws very rapidly, moves right back in his chair, brings up both hands in a defensive gesture with the palms flat out, blushes and shakes his head decisively): "Oh no, I couldn't stand that, that is just ... too much ..."

Energist: "Well clearly this is a shield made from energy and it is there to protect you from feeling what you just felt. Where did you feel that, I couldn't stand that, in your body?"

C (immediately indicates his throat with one hand and half a second later, with the other hand lower down on his central chest): "I'm not sure ..."

As we have noted before, at this point it is not safe to take the shield down – there is a serious problem with the channels somewhere in this gentleman's throat and chest. This example also nicely shows something you will notice time and time again in yourself and with others – the body knows immediately, the hands automatically indicate the location, but the conscious mind needs some time to figure out where it actually hurts. The longer someone takes to figure it out consciously, the more detached they have become from their own feedback devices which are designed to let you know when something is going wrong and action needs to be taken to put it right, or damage will result.

I sometimes ask people to "Freeze, don't move. Now, look at your own hands!" – and they are astonished to find their hands have already gone to the right place. This is a part of the personal experience with energy that EMO provides in practice and an important learning; our bodies know and they are trying to tell us not just where it hurts, but even how it could be healed.

The movements people make automatically when they engage in the healing process and when they encourage the energy flow through the channels, not just the stroking movements of the hands but all the other movements, are wonderful feedback devices that show us what goes on in their bodies and in their energy bodies.

Just looking at the ways in which people move with their own energy movements is very educational and opens not just the eyes to the reality of energy within us, all around us, and our physical reactions to those energy movements and occurrences.

Back with our client who had the big wall in front of his chest and head and injured ereas in this throat and chest which the shield was protecting,

Energist: "Which one hurts most, in the chest or in the throat?"

P (both hands immediately go to the chest): "In the chest, I feel very uncomfortable ..."

Energist: "Take a deep breath, and another one. That's very good.

"Now, this is only an energy, and it needs to flow away so that you can feel better. Keep on breathing deeply, that really helps.

"You keep your hands there, and I add my intention from the outside, and I want you to just stroke that place there where it hurts and say, "Soften and flow."

P (Nods, breathes deeply, hands making circular movements on the chest, breathes deeply again, seems to relax a little)

Energist: "Where does this energy need to go? There are natural channels for it and if we find the right ones, it can flow away."

P: "It needs to flow upwards, towards my throat. Now it hurts in my throat ..."

Energist: "That's very good, that was the second place we found. You're doing really well, that's right, stroke that place on your throat where it hurts and tell it to soften and flow. It's only an energy."

P (Nods)

Energist: "Keep breathing deeply and let that energy flow - where does it need to go from here?"

P (breathes deeply, hands stroking upwards towards the chin): "It needs to go up into my head."

Energist: "Excellent, that's very good. Soften and flow, this energy needs to find an exit point. What's happening?"

P (swallows, then swallows again, then yawns) "Oh it's in my head now, swirling around." (Takes a deep breath and starts moving his neck which had been extremely rigid for the first time in the session).

Energist: "That's excellent, by all means, move to assist the energy to find its right channel, find the exit point. Where does it need to go?"

P (now also moving shoulders and neck, hands on the top of the head): "It needs to come out of the top of my head."

Energist: "And can it go out?"

P: "Yes, yes, I can feel it, it's there, right on the top of my head, it's going out." (Blows out breath through pursed lips and starts to smile, still massaging the top of his head with his hands) "That feels so much better, like a relief, what a relief ..."

Energist: "Excellent job! You did that beautifully! Now, let's try that again from the beginning, look over the wall at your students, and this time if you can be ready when the energy comes in to help it move up and through the pathway we've just discovered, all the way in, through and out."

P: "Ok, so ... Oh. That's strange ..."

Energist: "What's happening?"

P: "It's like the wall ... it has shrunk? It's not as big as it was?"

Energist: "Can you show me with your hands?"

P (Indicates a smaller shield, from the brow of his head to the bottom of his chin, thinner and only about a foot square now). "That's so strange, it really has shrunk. Ok, I'm going to look over it now." (Cranes his neck as before and this time, takes a deep breath in, his hands go to his chest then quite quickly up to his throat and raise up before his face, then he exclaims, "Oh my God! I know what this is! I know where this comes from! I've just seen it, oh no, I never ..."

Energist: "What's happening? What did you see?"

P: "When I was a child, my father used to pick me up by the collar and lift me up of off the ground all the way up so I was in front of his face to shout at me, eye to eye, that's where it comes from, I remembered!"

Energist: "Wow, that's amazing! Of course, of course you would need a shield there to protect you!"

P (Very excited, speaking rapidly): "Yes, yes, that's exactly right, and that's why I made that barrier but I didn't know and it never came down and that's why I can't reach people now! I had no idea it was because of my father!"

Energist: "Can you take the shield down completely now? Do you think you can?"

P: "Yes, I'm going to be ready for when it hits me in the heart, I know what to do. I want the shield gone!"

Energist: (leans forward and makes direct eye contact, simulating the "incoming father energy")

P (Gasps, puts his hands on his chest, holds them there, then starts to laugh, "Oh my God! Oh that feels good! Like, like being struck by lightning but in a good way, it's rushing straight through, out the top of my head! Do you mind if I get up for a moment? I need to get up ..."

Energist: (Laughs, is delighted): "Yes by all means, you get up, all grown up now, stand tall ..."

P: "As tall now and taller than my father was back then ..."

This is a classic example which demonstrates many things you will find in the EMO process time and time again. The shield was very necessary to protect two major injuries from constantly flaring up, the one in the chest and the second one in the throat. There was also a third blockage, on the top of the head, but once the energy flow from beneath ramped up, this went away without further ado.

As the injury was repaired, the shield itself began to shrink in response; and with the improved energy flow came additional information, in this case the realisation where the injuries and the shield had come from in the first place.

It was the final test however that brought on the real EMO Energized End State with the realisation that now he was grown up and taller than his father had ever been.

This is invaluable information for this gentleman; and now, his energy system working as it should again, he can stand in front of his students as a powerful grown man who wants to help them, not cause them injury as had happened to him when he was small.

Following this session, the gentleman had many more insights and also expressed a real admiration for his younger aspect who did manage to protect himself from his father's energetic transgressions by building the shield - even the child had not been as helpless as he had previously thought.

140

Of course, for the EMO process it is not necessary to know the details of the genesis of the problem and how it manifested across time; but it is very true that cause-and-effect relationships become apparent in the course of doing EMO that can have the intensity of revelations, as entire life systems all of a sudden become known and understood.

Clarity, huge cognitive changes and conscious understanding which results from renewal in the energy body is something that in my opinion is one of the most profound proofs that the underlying theory of EMO is entirely sound and works with the realities of human organisation across energy-neurology-physicality. This clarity and understanding is also something you can look forward to experiencing as the whys and wherefores of your own problems become revealed to you.

Here are the basics about shields once more in brief.

Shields In Brief

- You know a shield exists when there is a powerful incoming energy form but no corresponding body sensation happens, or only a generalised vague feeling of pressure is felt.

- Shields also result in a general feeling of "being disconnected" from any topic, person or occurrence.

- People have an energy mind which knows where the shields are and can show us with the person's hands the location and shape of the shield.

- We make a tiny hole into the shield to let a little bit of the energy in question flow in.

- This helps us discover the reason for the shield – the energetic injury or disturbance behind the shield.

- We heal the injury behind the shield as per normal using the same EMO protocol we use for all energetic injuries, blockages and disturbances.

- We test how well the healed system is working by sending the energy form again, and consecutively making the hole/s in the shield larger, or the shield more transparent.

- When the energetic injury is entirely healed, the shield disappears automatically or is simply removed by the owner of the shield.

Energy Relationships

Energy Allergies

Working with shields, we made an interesting discovery.

This is expressed in the EMO statement of,

"There is no good or bad energy – there is ONLY ENERGY."

To many people who are new to energy work this seems an extraordinary and highly controversial statement – surely, there are all sorts of negative energies against which we must shield ourselves?

This is what we have heard, what we have been taught, and of course, we have all experienced incidences of being in the presence of "negative energy" and how this has affected us.

However, once you start doing EMO for a while and with a number of different people, it turns out that we misinterpreted something that really happens.

A classic example is a person who is suffering from the effects of negative energy being sent their way by someone who they dislike.

This energy "feels bad" and "hurts".

One EMO session later, and the correct channels having being found and activated for this energy form, and it no longer feels bad at all – in the contrary, the person is highly energized by the same energy form, experiences this energy form as actively nutritious.

This happens over and over again when you do EMO with people - "negative energy" stops being experienced as "negative" and becomes **ONLY ENERGY** instead when the pain stops.

We were surprised at first, but with hindsight, it makes perfect sense.

People are designed to live on this planet, and with other people.

143

They are also designed to live with the energetic occurrences that surround us.

We are made to function, survive and thrive in this world and in the proverbial oceans of energy.

There are no "bad" or "negative" things in nature at all. All of nature is interdependent, and as we have already noted, a maggot may not be as cute as a baby kitten, but that doesn't make the maggot negative, or any worse, or any less beloved by the Creative Order.

We have found that people experience entirely innocent energy forms as "negative" **because they hurt**.

And the energy form only hurts because of an injury or malfunction in the human energy body which is designed to channel **all** occurring energy forms we may encounter on this planet in our lifetimes.

In EMO, we think of negative energy in terms of someone having an energy allergy if they feel that this one particular energy form is negative or painful to them.

Here we meet for the first time in EMO the human ability to influence and change energetic realities head on.

People make judgements – and **judgements create shields**.

A person might for example declare that red is a very bad colour and that it hurts; that blue makes them sad, grey is soothing and peaceful, green is good and yellow even better, but black entirely unacceptable because it is so negative, and pink must never be mentioned at all.

The simple fact is that there are no good or bad colours; there are only colours.

Once we approach energy occurrences in that way, by reminding us that there is no good or bad energy, **only energy** and our responses to that, we can take a totally different tack to a range of old

144

problems that significantly influence how many different kinds of nutrients our energy body gets to receive.

In our simple colour example, we can see that this person's energy body is missing out on certain vibrations, existences, experiences and a whole range of energy forms which have been made "bad" and placed out of bounds, shielded against.

Colours are everywhere and in every thing; when we reject pink, we might also ending up rejecting a pink rose, or a pink diamond, a pink sunset or a seashell, or a piglet, or a person who wears pink or lives in a pink house, or a white person's pink skin …

All those things get removed from the energy body nutritional menu by rejecting pink.

People do this all the time, very thoughtlessly.

Some reject nature; some reject concrete car parks instead.

Both miss out on the actual energy present in their environment.

This energy does not only provide real and actual energy for life; it goes further than that, because the energy flow in, through and out the energy body also carries with it important information about the world around us.

You can say that anything we consciously reject and put up a shield against impoverishes not just our physical systems, which are absolutely reliant on a good functioning energy body behind the scenes, but also our emotional systems, as we don't get to experience these "other" feelings from these other energy forms; and very importantly, we don't get enough information to make good assessments and decisions, or think clearly and logically.

The realisation that the energy flow between our energy bodies and all the energy forms in the environment is not just about having a healthy, well fed energy body and fully functional energy immune system, but that energy also carries information, was amazing, and wonderful both.

Of course!

We can only learn about things that we experience ourselves – and we experience our environment not just through the usual five senses, but also through the 6th sense, the felt sensations from the energy body, which provides the energy mind with this incredible amount of additional information.

We call this …

The Energy Of Learning

When we create shields to reject certain incoming energies that we have judged to be bad energies, we close the door on learning something else about this energy, and lose an important jig saw puzzle piece we need to make sense of the world.

The oceans of energy become a fish tank.

When we start to experiment with deliberately opening ourselves up to things, people, existences that were previously deemed to be bad, negative or painful, that is when the truth of the world as being this totally amazing place begins to reveal itself.

In every EMO session we notice just how much learning happens when the general flow of energy through the energy body is increased, and never more so than when energy forms that were previously kept at bay finally can run smoothly through a person's systems.

This happens over and over again; a person who might have been terrified of spiders, once their injuries are healed and they have tasted the spider energy, removed the shields step by step, and has an EMO Energized End State with that which previously terrified them, will have an endless stream of insights about spiders, their value, their existence, and how much they *admire* these marvellous creatures.

We have all heard tales how we are "all interconnected in the vast web of life" but taking down shields to a specific energy form and experiencing for yourself just how much more you end up knowing about that energy form, about that existence, and how much it "broadens your horizons" makes being a part of the web of life into an actual experienced reality.

That's pretty awesome and if you wanted to, you could develop this into a lifetime's hobby, simply finding things you previously thought were bad or negative, removing your shields and injuries and learning something about these things in the most amazing way.

The energy of learning is an experience like no other; it comes free of charge as people seek to heal their painful injuries and start to work with energy and emotion in a whole new way.

In its own right, the energy of learning is a wondrous topic and one that I think you will find has many applications, and will bring you much joy.

Enlightening Cognition

We have already touched on the idea that the movement of energy through the energy body changes cognition and affects beliefs, values and attitudes.

I also made the comment that this is one of the tests of the underlying theory as far as I am concerned that EMO makes real, structural changes to the totality which includes how a person thinks.

The EMO process changes beliefs, values, attitudes and impacts cognition directly; one of the most fascinating manifestations of this are the enlightenment insights people report during and after an EMO experience.

The human neurology and the cause-and-effects of someone's personality, problem groups and interlinkages, memories of experiences past and present, wishes, hopes and fears for the future are a multidimensional matrix with layers and levels so complex that the greatest supercomputer could not begin to unravel this.

The human totality, on the other hand, is exactly designed to compute this multi-dimensional complexity. This is why we have "more neurons in our brains than there are stars in the visible sky and the connections between them, are to all intents and purposes, infinite". And that's just the physical brain alone ...

We really do not need such brains and systems for computing n-complexity in order to dig for roots; and the simple reason that we only use a minute percentage of our brain capacity is because it is there for computing multi-ordinate, n-complex systems in the oceans of energy.

To read energy systems correctly is a natural ability with which everyone is born and everyone can do this, if they want to – and if their energy systems are flowing freely because these energies do not just carry "life energy" and "nutrients" but indeed, they carry

149

information of such density and complexity, it is breathtaking and entirely unimaginable in terms of data storage in the mechanical systems we are familiar with.

We have already observed how five minutes of EMO gave people understandings of how their problems originated in a fantastically logical fashion that they most likely would have taken many years in therapy to arrive at – if ever they had been able to arrive at these insights at all.

Following the experience of the EMO Energized End State, new cognitive insights and connections literally pour forth from the person who had the experience; it is fascinating to observe, and even more fascinating to experience how energy flow and information flow seem to be one and the same.

Take out an energy blockage without knowing what it is about, and all of a sudden, huge areas of a person's life start to make sense.

Here is an example of such a profound insight.

This client C was seeking weight reduction for health purposes and was working on a sensation of strong hunger pangs which would arise spontaneously and then she would have to eat large amounts of bulky (starchy) foods in order to make those hunger pangs go away. These "hunger pangs" when the stomach was full already are also classed as emotions in EMO, falling under the heading of "a physical sensation that does not have a physical origin."

As is the case with many other EMO clients, this lady had already received much therapy, counselling and coaching which had not impacted the problem at all.

We pick up the story just after the EMO Master Practitioner has asked where in her body she feels these hunger pangs, and to show this with her hands.

C (puts hands on large stomach, fingers spread wide apart): "I feel it right here. It really is painful."

150

Energist: "Well, let us consider the energy there. Where does it want to go?"

C: "There is an upward pressure."

Energist: "Let it flow and gently encourage it to go upward, tell me what's happening as you do it, please."

C: "It is going up my chest, between my breasts, into my throat and ... oh ... oh I don't believe it ...oh no ..." (starts to cry softly)

Energist: "What happened?"

C (crying silently): "I know what the hunger is, the emptiness I'm trying to fill. There should be babies in there."

This client was truly shocked and absolutely at a loss to explain why she never even thought of this before; she had three grown children and consciously, never once expected to be wanting any more. The session developed into an understanding that when this lady had felt her babies move inside her stomach during pregnancy, she had felt "not alone" for the only time in her life and now, when she felt alone, "the hunger pangs" would arrive.

What is so fascinating about this process and the cognitive repercussions is that with hindsight, it is totally logical and absolutely understandable, yet would never have been discovered by "talking with the head" at all because in her head, she was absolutely congruent that she didn't want any more children and was perfectly satisfied with the three she already had.

The truth is simply that we cannot solve all our problems with the kind of communication we are used to – not between each other, not within ourselves and not with the universe at large. Talking with linear language and thinking linear thoughts gets us next to nowhere in the realms of a totality that is made of energy, of physicality and of conscious thought that can affect the very fabric of reality absolute.

The breakthrough cognitions that go with EMO make a re-connection between all layers of the totality and that is a very important aspect of working with EMO.

For example, in this lady's case now there is compassion for the aspects of her that suggest a solution to the problem of "being alone;" her eating behaviours make total sense and there is no longer a war between the various parts of consciousness, neurology and physiology. Even if the problem of "energy collapse due to loneliness" had not been resolved by taking the session to the EMO Energized End State, where the client felt in her body that she was not alone, that she was always connected to the universe and her children as well as God itself in the session afterwards, a very different state of understanding and congruency in the self would have been achieved.

To have the correct information about occurrences in the oceans of energy is of course, a prime requisite of being able to function successfully, to survive without damage and to be able to take action in response to the environment that will work.

Fighting loneliness (read "disconnection from the universe at large") with calorie counting doesn't work; it doesn't bring the correct results, it really is as simple as that. It leads to chaos and even more disturbances. Relieving the energetic blockages that create the sensation of loneliness, on the other hand, brings about immediate cessation of both that as well as ending the well-meaning yet futile attempts to firstly, have to have a baby in the stomach to not feel alone for a while, and then, to try and replace babies with carbohydrates to create a similar body sensation.

The concept of **energy as a carrier for information** is probably one of the most exciting and most fascinating aspects of the EMO process once we get beyond mere emergency treatments.

Learning "With The Heart"

The Yellow Emperor notes that "You learn with your heart and you process with the head."

I am sure I don't have to tell you how the 1st World learning and teaching methods have that particular rat hanging upside down by the tail entirely – you have been to school, you know what it is like when you are sitting there and try to stuff dusty nonsense into your head when your heart and all the rest of you is yearning to be elsewhere.

That is systemically so appalling that words truly fail me.

There are even suggestions that "if you can make the material interesting, the students retention rate increases significantly".

Wake up "the heart" just a little and a little is learned; learn with "the heart" directly and all is learned, then we can process in the head afterwards.

When you open yourself to the world and take in the energy of a thing, you learn about that thing in a whole new way.

This is true multi-dimensional, multi-modality, experiential learning which includes the information and energy we receive through our sixth sense and which we can physically feel flowing through our bodies when we pay attention.

So, for example, if you wish to become a geologist, energetically speaking the right approach would be to spend time with rocks, open yourself to these rocks and let their energy flow into you, bringing with it all you need to know about the nature of rocks. When you have done that and not before, you can begin what the First World wrongly terms "study," which is looking at the head stuff – chemical composition, maps of where they occur, formation and such.

That way around, you will be a first class geologist who will contribute significantly to the collection of human head knowledge about rocks; chances are you will be able to add some very surprising insights and additional findings about rocks that "came from nowhere" and they will hail you as a genius in geologist circles.

The same applies for every field of human endeavour – there are levels of learning, of knowing, of understanding which are way, way above and beyond book learning.

When you begin to work with "the energy of learning" for yourself and in this way, you will probably encounter energy blockages on the topic of study and learning that have arisen because of the wrongful ways learning is being handled systemically and the terrible experiences we have all had, leading to totally damaged self constructs believing that they are stupid, that they cannot learn, that they cannot learn to understand because they have failed to arrange arbitrary two dimensional symbols in the "correct" order and linear sequence.

Here is an exercise you can do for yourself and simply note, like a true scientist and explorer, what happens when you do.

The EMO Rock Me Exercise

1. Find a rock.

2. Put the rock on a table and sit, looking at it. Relax and breathe freely and deeply.

3. Where can you feel that rock in your body? Show me with your hands.

4. Where does the energy from the rock want to go? Allow it to come in and find the requisite channels.

5. Allow the rock energy to flow into you, through you and out.

6. Keep it up until you have a steady flow between you and the rock that needs no further conscious attention but runs naturally by itself.

7. Allow the energy flow to speed up, to become faster and until you have reached the EMO Energized End State of feeling tingly and alive.

8. Take a moment to reflect on what you have learned thanks to the rock, then you can put it back where you found it.

This is the basic EMO protocol for "learning through energy and information".

This form of learning through the energy of a thing has been reserved for shamans, priests, healers and their apprentices throughout the ages, the very best people of the tribe.

A hundred thousand years ago it may have been so that only the very best people could learn this way – now, we all have the neurology to just that. It is time that custom got in sync with genetic evolution and tribal habits caught up with reality – and that reality is that we can all learn to understand not just rocks but trees, animals and even other people on that level.

Wisdom Learning

Now, go out and learn. All it needs is to firstly, consciously becoming aware of any blockages, shields, barriers to receiving the energy from (the tree, the cat, the plant, the grass, the earth, the sky, the night, the moon, etc. ad infinitum) and to dissolve them so that the energy may flow freely through the requisite pathways and enter our energy bodies. In doing so, these energies will be like "the hand that passes across the clay tablet;" the incoming energy forms interact and change your energy system as they pass through them. Thus, the learnings will become yours, a part of you absolutely – they can never be forgotten, they cannot be undone and no-one can ever take them away from you.

I cannot tell you what that feels like nor what that does for you as a person; you will have to go out and experience it for yourself.

Keep doing it, and remember that the true object of the EMO exercise is to put this whole happening on automatic pilot so that you don't have to think about it any longer. So that when you are in the presence of something you want to know better and feel more connected with, understand on a visceral level of having true experience of it, your energy system automatically corrects the blockages to this energy because it has learned that is what you want and need it to do.

Once you have found the courage and conviction to be doing this consciously, we can move on to a particularly interesting form of energy learning – learning from people.

Learning From People

The so called "pyramid of human learning" which refers to book learning or head learning rather than experience which is what learning with energy straight into our energy bodies could be called has through the millennia (and still does today on a massive scale!) suffered from the Chinese Whispers problem.

I have much experience with the evolution of a field beyond the person who originated it in the first place.

What happens regular as clockwork is that a person discovers or develops something that brings about truly amazing results when they do it. Students flock to them in order to learn how to do the same; but they don't and what was a "clear blue field" of something or other that was amazingly effective becomes eroded with every teaching and learning generation away from the originator until, within a few short years, it becomes entirely unrecognisable as what it used to be and muddy, diluted, and basically ineffective.

It is my supposition that this happens because the students don't allow the energy from the teacher to become a part of them and to change them so that they may learn to do the same as the teacher did.

When I put forth the proposition that in order to really, really learn from any teacher, one would have to open up entirely to them and allow their energy to run into you, through you and out, and allow it to structurally change you, people simply freak out. But – would we not be poisoned by them and all their shortcomings? Would we not become their slaves? Fall in love with them? Never have another original thought of our own? Inherit their limitations and make the same mistakes?

Try it for yourself. For what its worth, whenever I have done it, I have come away loving the person indeed. I have understood them in a way that I cannot explain in words, and I have been completely aware of their limitations and disturbances as a result, allowing me

157

to move their explorations on without having to destroy them or thinking of myself as being better as they are. I also understood their materials and explanations perfectly and moreover, what they were teaching and how they were trying to teach it made perfect sense to me.

Looking at the words someone speaks or writes is one information set; but if you put that together with the energy of learning and all that extra information about the teacher and all the things they didn't even knew themselves they knew, you really do get a much richer, more inclusive education that can be further evolved easily.

I highly recommend this and would now say that any course of study that doesn't take the energy of the teacher or originator or both into consideration is quite incomplete.

Energy, Information & Love

We have noted that when the energy flow increases, more information becomes accessible, to the degree that I now use energy and information interchangeably.

At the same time, we do have the phenomenon that increased energy flow also causes an increase in good feelings – and a result of those good feelings of expansion, aliveness, connectedness and understanding is that people naturally start to talk about love.

The three seem to be inextricably linked, if not simply different sides of a three sided coin.

If you increase energy flow, you increase information, and when you increase information flow, love increases too.

Now this is not some kind of spiritual make belief or religious notion; it is a structural fact of working with EMO that repeats over, and over, and over again as many times as you might want to observe it, with as many different kinds of people as you'd like to try it with, on as many different and seemingly impossible topics as you could bring to the table.

The increase in energy flow that is also an increase in information and in love is entirely structural.

This is the answer to the questions that are always asked about EMO, especially about that movement that takes us from deeply negative and painful emotions beyond the zero point of peace and into the positive emotions of joy and of love:

"I hate spiders! It is impossible I could ever learn to love a spider! It is inconceivable, it can't be done ..."

"I hate my perpetrators! They are evil! I know my religion says I should love them but it is impossible, it is inconceivable, it can't be done ..."

"I hate that other tribe of people over there! They are not even human! They have killed my people, they are behaving worse than animals, there can be no forgiveness, never mind love, it is inconceivable, it can't be done ..."

The tragedy is that from the 1st person standpoint it all feels so true, because it is true in that state.

From that desperately painful and disturbing state of stuck energies, injuries and reversals, you couldn't possibly feel or think or say anything else.

Yet with EMO it happens over and over again, predictably and every time, that if you heal the blockages and injuries and restore the Even Flow, the person ends up not just feeling better about that which they previously hated and rejected with all their heart, but also that they now understand much more, and if the energy flow ramps up enough, they will end up having an experience of unconditional love for that which only moments ago was a threat, a mortal enemy, an evil thing they would have destroyed that had been in their power to do so.

Real unconditional love isn't a vague religious concept; it is **a structural reality** that happens naturally in human beings when they work as they were designed to work in the first place, when there is a powerful flow of energy and information through the systems.

This is awesome on one hand; on the other, it is a huge, huge challenge to the people who are still in pain and from their 1st person perspective feel in every fibre of their being, that it is their right and duty to hate, reject and seek to destroy.

People who have had no personal experience yet of that natural occurrence that is the Even Flow of energy, information and love have all sorts of wrong ideas about what it might be like to live on the other side of that zero point of peace.

160

They will hallucinate in the absence of personal experience that "loving the perpetrator" might mean it's ok to rape small children, or that they would feel nothing about that any longer, or that they would no longer be motivated to fight against the evils of child abuse.

Nothing could be further from the truth, but unless you've been there and visited with that unknown territory on the other side of the zero point of peace, you simply cannot know.

All we can do here is to say to someone who is still in that 1st person position of it being simply inconceivable that what they hate could be loved, should be loved and if it was, everything would change, "Trust in the structure."

"Trust the fact that additional energy flow is the right way to go; that more information is better than less information, that more energy for life is better than less energy for life, and that more experience of love is better than less experience of love."

Now I have talked here of high end challenges to the energy -> information -> love principle, such as a spider phobia, child abuse and racial hatred; but we don't have to start there.

Test the theory and the structure of EMO on something small, and test it often.

You or a client might "hate" to clean the toilet, or to mow the lawn. Can this hate be turned to love by softening and flowing a few blockages here and there and improving the flow of energy through the body?

Is it really possible to love cleaning the toilet, or mowing the lawn?

Wouldn't you like to find out for yourself, experience in your own body, whether what all the prophets of the ages have been preaching about unconditional love is actually really true?

That unconditional love doesn't actually heal, but that loving is what we do naturally when we have become healed?

161

Pick something you hate. Something small, like doing your taxes or cleaning out the cat litter.

Use EMO and find out for yourself.

Don't delay.

Personal experience of the interchangeable nature of energy, information and love is priceless and will quite practically transform your incarnation for the better – and by extension, the incarnations of those you touch.

All The World Your Teacher

I have met many people who were seeking a or even THE teacher, the one who would bring them to enlightenment and who would show them the way out of their own personal darkness into paradise on Earth.

I understand now that they were nearly on the right track – and nearly there (dicht daneben ist auch vorbei!) can be more frustrating by far than just not even being anywhere close to this idea at all.

The thing is that if you consider the forms of learning we have been talking about, it would be madness to put the burden of evolving you towards enlightenment on the frail shoulders of a single human being.

To learn about the universe, of course we need to learn about all the universe – including our humble rock, the clouds and sand. Plants, insects, animals. Weather, time and space.

And other people can teach us too but we need not just one person to become our teacher.

We need *all of them*.

Everyone can be your teacher, and the more you open yourself to that without fear and nothing but the deep desire to learn (and because it is such an amazing experience that feels so good!) the more you learn and the more experienced you become.

I call learning that is based on personal experience (as opposed to having read something in a book) wisdom learning.

If you dare to learn, you can learn the most amazing things from a tramp in the street, from that annoying little old lady who is holding up the queue in the supermarket because she is trying to have a conversation with the bored check out assistant, from that droning, boring politician, from that low class urban layabout petty criminal, from that redneck army sergeant, from that scary gangsta, from the downtrodden, worn out mother-of-five and from every one of her unique children and babies – from *everyone*.

When you let the energy of a person flow into you, through you and out and allow it to change you to give you that additional energy, information and love, what you will be learning is not just about their limitations but about *the human condition*.

You could say that each and every person has something to teach you that you didn't know about yet, something precious and unique that you might have never expected to know at all.

However, I appreciate that this is advanced people learning. You might want to start by just dropping all remaining barriers to your favourite teacher, someone you feel comfortable with and who has inspired you. You can evoke them by playing a video tape, an audio tape, bring out a book they wrote or look at a picture of the person.

Then, it is only a matter of the basic EMO process and for you open yourself wide and say, "Teach me."

And perhaps the thought, deep in the back of your mind, that ...

"My heart is as open as the sky."

PART 3 - EMO ENERGY EXERCISES

Paying Attention To Energy Sensations

This is a very easy exercise for absolute EMO beginners. It really does teach us a lot about paying attention to energy sensations; and with a bit of practice this is something you can do at any time to brighten your day.

This is also a superb exercise which can transform the experience of sex with a partner, or by yourself.

1. Touch or have another touch you lightly with one fingertip on the arm or some other part of your body.

2. Have them lightly massage or tap the area.

3. Follow the sensation of the touch as it travels through your system with your intention.

4. Trace sensation as it travels the path all the way from the touch, through your body, and find the natural exit point/s.

5. Encourage the speed of the movement of energy until it is so fast from touch to exit that it feels like a miniature lightning strike or a flash.

6. Notice how alive it makes you feel and repeat by trying this on a different part of your body.

This is a great practice exercise for EMO and really wakes up your energy body; you can do this at any time you need a lift, to gain extra energy and to change your emotions.

The Basic EMO Emotion Healing Exercise

- Call up an old emotion you know well and which you can feel in your body.

- Where do you feel this in your body? Show me with your hands.

- Place your hands, your healing hands and your attention there and consider where this energy needs to go.

- Think and say, "This is only an energy! Soften and flow!"

- Pay attention to where this energy needs to go. Breathe deeply, don't overthink this. Watch your hands as they move, they can often give a clue where the energy needs to go. If it feels painful, the energy needs to soften more. Massage the erea with your healing hands as you think and say, "This is only an energy - soften and flow ..."

- Once the energy starts to move, you need to find the exit point. If you lose track of the energy flow, remind yourself of the original erea and the problem to re-start the energy flow and discover the pathway the energy needs to take to find its way out.

- Encourage yourself and the energy flow by breathing deeply, allowing natural body movements to assist you, using your healing hands of energy and also by saying to yourself when the energy starts to move, "That's very good! Soften and flow!"

- When you have the pathway established, re-call the original experience and repeat moving the energy in, through and out, until it flows instantly and cleanly, and the original 'emotional pain' is no more.

- Now encourage the energy to move faster and faster until you experience an exciting, electric, pleasurable, charging sensation which we call the EMO Energized End State.

- Take a moment to think back on the original experience and notice what new information and insights you have gained as a result of the EMO process.

Well done!

Here are some important tips from experience with EMO in self help.

Be gentle with yourself and don't give up too easily. Don't presume that just because you found other or older energy methods difficult, this one will be too. EMO is really easy and natural. Soften and flow!

Notice if you get wound up or stressed, or when your body locks up "in furious concentration" and you're trying way too hard. Relax! Breathe! Move a little. Remind yourself out aloud that this is only an energy, we all have energy bodies and healing hands of energy, and if you're a human being, you can learn to do this too.

If you are having trouble with the basic EMO exercise, don't worry. Have a go at the other exercises, especially the daily exercises which you do in real life, as and when it happens. We are not learning anything artificial here, we are simply re-activating systems we were all born with.

Most importantly - even a little movement in an old stuck problem is real progress for someone who is trying this for the first time. Celebrate that and build on it. Be a good coach to yourself, encourage yourself, keep a positive attitude especially at the beginning, and remind yourself that practice makes perfect!

The Energy Nutrition Exercise

1. Find any object, person, plant, fruit, animal, landscape, music, work of art, weather, etc. and tune into its energy.

2. Drop any shields you might have to this 'incoming energy'.

3. Where do you feel it in your body?

4. Where does it need to go?

5. Assist in flowing it freely through its requisite channels, all the way through and out.

6. Ramp up the energy flow until you feel tingly, electric, happy, alive.

7. Take a moment to reflect what you have gained by the way of additional energy, information and love.

With just a little practice, EMO gets better and better.

EMO is wonderful, especially when shared with friends, so enjoy discovering your own personal connection to the Oceans of Energy.

The Superfast EMO Anti-Stress Meditation

This quick mini-meditation against stress is excellent for people who don't know what EMO is to give them a very fast personal experience of what it feels like to pay attention to the flow of energy in the body. For people who do know what EMO is, this exercise provides instant stress relief, just as the title promises, any time you start to feel the first signs of stress in your body.

We came up with this exercise at an international mind, body, spirit festival where my publishing company had a book stand, and there were quite a few other EMO people who had come to visit. We found it really useful when people asked, "What is EMO?" instead of talking about it, to say, "Here, let us show you ..."

Over the four days we were there, hundreds of people had their first EMO experience - and they loved it.

You can do this exercise any time, anywhere and with just about anyone and really noticeable stress relief is achieved. Remember to increase the flow of energy until it starts to tingle and feel exciting at the end, that's when we go beyond the zero point of peace and into the EMO Energized End State where it feels good!

1. We all carry our stress in our bodies - that's where we put it, that's where it becomes a burden, and those are the places where illness can take hold.

2. Take a deep breath and pay attention to your body for a moment. Where do you carry the worst of your stress? Which part of your body feels the most tight, tense, heavy, locked up?

3. Put your hands there now or just point so we know exactly where this stress spot is located.

4. Now simply feel that you are standing under an energy shower, and pleasant energy is falling down onto that stressed erea, beginning to soften it up, beginning to make it flow, down and away, stuck energy softening up and flowing through the channels that were designed to carry this energy away.

5. Feel it flowing down those channels and all the way out of your body.

6. Move a little, if you will; use your hands to massage the erea a little to help the energy flow all the way, through and out, and breathe deeply.

7. Now let the energy flow faster in, through and all the way out, a fast rushing of energy like a waterfall to clear out all the remaining stress and until you feel happy and tingly inside and out.

Well done - and pay attention to stress feelings in your body from now so you can do a little EMO right away to keep you energized and flowing. You can do this at any time, anywhere, and the more you remember to do this, the better you get at instant stress relief, using nothing but the real feelings in your body that tell you where you carry your stress, and a little attention to encourage the flow of energy.

Greeting The Day, Greeting The Night

This is a beautiful and very moving exercise that benefits you in many more ways than you might suspect just yet. Do the exercise for a week and you will begin to know just how much support and sustenance there is for us - simply by virtue of being here. It is also a training exercise to teach us about the energetic realities of giving and receiving energies and to give us practice at working equally confidently with either form of flow.

Since I first created this exercise, a decade has passed and I couldn't tell you on how many occasions this simple energy movement brightened my day and gave me energy for both day and night, so I commend it to you personally and highly indeed.

Greeting The Day

Step outside as soon as you have risen and open yourself to the World. Take a moment to breathe deeply and then say, "Day, I greet you."

Allow this day - rainy or bright, cold or hot, no matter what - to come to you, to bring you its totally unique properties, for not one day is ever quite the same as the day before, nor all the days to follow; allow this day to give you its own unique energy and information.

State your intention to receive this unique energy into all your systems, and now pay attention to any physical responses you might be having to this enterprise. Any emotions, where they localised? Place your hand there and soften the sensation, until the energy there runs clearly in all ways. Any sensations of pressure, discomfort, nervousness, any sensations of rejecting this day at all, localise them and make them run smoothly.

One more time, re-state the words, "Day, I greet you." Remain with this for just a few moments, then thank the day for its unique gifts on this occasion and step back inside and into your ordinary life.

Greeting The Night

When the night has fallen, step outside.

Take a moment to look around, to get into rapport with the night and become a little more still and a little more observant, and then say, "Night, I greet you."

As before, check yourself for any physiological sensations or emotions which might denote an underlying energy blockage that stops a true exchange of energies between you and the night on this occasion.

Especially, look for any "stuck" energy that might have accumulated during the day in your dealings in the Hard and soften this, allowing the night to take away whatever is no longer needed, drawing all this up and into its endless self.

Give the night everything you need to give, really allow it to draw from you your energetic burdens, your unexpressed stale energies, anything at all – your love, your loneliness, your unfulfilled desires. The beautiful night will take it all.

Allow this process to complete - it can be as swift as a thought, that is entirely up to you.

Give a sincere "Thank You" to the night for its assistance and its lessons and then return to your normal activities at this time.

These exercises take just a few moments of your time each day but in energetic terms, they are truly profound and most balancing, soothing, healing and energising.

You will notice that with even two or three repetitions, your ability to channel energy from the day and night increases dramatically as your systems and their pathways are becoming clearer and more efficient. To begin with, you might strongly "take from the day" and "release to the night."

As time goes by you will find that indeed, for both the day and the night what is happening is a spiral energy exchange of giving and taking in equal measure, as each have their own unique lessons and energies to give, as well as assisting you in taking what is no longer needed.

It is a beautiful and very moving exercise that benefits you in many more ways than you might suspect just yet.

Do the exercise for a week and you will begin to know just how much energy support and sustenance there is for us - simply by virtue of being here.

Mother Earth & Father Sky Exercise

This is a traditional energy exercise which, when you involve EMO, becomes a profound and very real experience of grounding and charging all at the same time.

It goes all the way back to 2002 when I was trying to teach EMO to a very sceptical audience which even contained some people who refused to acknowledge that they had ever felt any kind of emotion before. I took them out into the gardens, did this exercise with the group and it changed their minds as the powerful energies of Mother Earth & Father Sky came to my rescue on the day and taught even the sceptics the reality of energy by personal experience.

This exercise is also a good example of how many traditional energy exercises can be brought to life when you add EMO to the mix and take the time to really pay attention to the sensations of energy movements we can feel in our physical bodies.

1. Stand comfortably and pay attention to the sensations in your feet, legs and your entire body. Move a little to become more comfortable and loosen any tight parts of your body.

2. Take a deep breath and pay attention to the earth on which you are standing.

3. Feel the energy from the earth as it flows into you and up your body, all the way in, through and out.

4. Let the energy flow fast and powerfully without hindrance to help lift you.

How does that feel?

Very good. Now:

5. Stand comfortably, take a deep breath and pay attention to the sky which is above us.

6. Feel the energy from the sky flow down and into you, through you and out your feet, all the way in, through and out.

7. Let the energy flow fast and powerfully without hindrance to ground you.

And now:

8. Take a deep breath and let the energies from Mother Earth & Father Sky move together, at the same time, lifting you and grounding you, moving through your energy body as they take their paths, feel their Even Flow, their rhythm and life.

This is an excellent energy exercise which can also be used to lift and ground respectively at any time as well as both together which are more than the sum of their parts.

The Healing Sun Exercise

This exercise comes from an experience I had with a group of civil war survivors in an East European country who had known only appalling personal injury, heartbreak from multiple bereavements, torture and mistreatment, hunger and loss, and little hope of joy for the future left.

As there were no beautiful gardens there, no trees left which had all been chopped up for fire wood, broken roads and only ruins all about us, I looked around in desperation to find something and there I found the sun in the sky. So I used this powerful energy source for an EMO experience with these people.

Their response was amazing - many started to cry for the first time, they came to life and at the end one lady told me, "You have given me the sunshine back - how can I ever thank you?"

This was a profoundly moving experience for me also and it created this simple EMO exercise which can also be used for self help "when the worst has come to the worst."

1. Find the sun. You can go outside or do this inside through a window.

2. Find the place in your body where it hurts the most. Put your hands there.

3. Now turn your body so that the sun shines on that place. You can feel the warmth of the sun on the back of your hands; this will let you know when you are in the right position if you are wearing a lot of clothes.

4. Slowly move your hands away and let the energy from the sun directly warm and heal that erea.

5. With your intention, simply think/say at the same time, "Soften and flow."

6. Pay attention to the sensations as the sun energy begins to flow in, through and out of your energy body and you can feel this with your physical body.

7. When you are ready, open yourself entirely to the sun healing and let the energy flow through as fast as it will.

8. Keep the sun energy flowing until you don't feel sad any longer but indeed, amazingly alive and blessed.

The EMO Energy Dancing Exercise

Energy dancing with EMO is a fabulous experience and it can be used for self help especially, with the music providing the focus and the rhythms providing additional energy input.

Your EMO partner in Energy Dancing is your own body.

You can use music that strongly evokes an emotional response, such as "this song always makes me cry because it reminds me of ..." and we also have special Energy Dancing programs to work with various emotional problems now.

For this exercise, we are simply going to focus on something that is a big emotional stressor in your life right now, and you can feel this in your body.

1. Pick some music to help you de-stress, something with a good, strong beat and a powerful rhythm that will help you move and let the energy flow.

2. Where do you feel the most stress in your body? Show yourself with your hands.

3. Now start to move and sway a little with the beat of the music and let your spine find the right movements to help flow more energy to that place of stress.

4. Move your hips and your legs to help improve the energy flow. Pay attention how the movement is helping with the energy flow through your body and how that feels.

5. Move your feet and toes, your knees as well to help with the energy flow.

6. Now, start moving your head, neck and shoulders, your arms and your fingers too, your face, your eyebrows, your eyes, your mouth and tongue, even your nose until all of you is dancing, all of you is helping that place where you feel your stress the most.

7. Breathe deeply and enjoy as you get into it and the energy in your body flows faster and faster, and you are feeling more and more sparkly, electric and alive.

8. When the music ends, jump up and give yourself a round of applause - you've just had your first experience of EMO Energy Dancing!

Once you can do the basics of energy dancing, you can use it in many different ways, and at any time there is music.

One gentleman told us of driving home late at night, being very tired and stressed, worrying about the safety of his driving when it occurred to him to put the radio on and use the music to relieve and release all the many stress feelings and feelings of tiredness, one after the other. The tiredness went away as "if by magic," he felt energized, fresh and drove home swiftly and confidently, helped along by the music. He reports that by the time he got home, he had plenty of energy to really great his wife and they had a wonderful night together.

I had a personal experience of teaching a training in a hot country - incredibly hot, over 45' centigrade, and now it was late and I was so exhausted, I wanted to cry. On the way back to the hotel, I stopped off at a street cafe' just to rest and because I couldn't take another step; there, some quite terrible music was blaring through tinny speakers into the night. As I'd taught EMO Energy Dancing to the group earlier in the day, it came to my mind; could this work here, with this appalling music? And indeed it did. I just moved lightly on my bar stool, soften and flowed, and not five minutes later I was sparkling and had an excellent evening followed by a superb night's sleep as well.

Another lady told of a transformational experience she had at a New Year's Eve party, shortly after her EMO practitioner training. She was "made to dance" by her partner and became aware of many painful sensations in her body - about not being young enough to dance in public any longer, about making a fool of herself, about moving too sexually and not age appropriate, about her clothes not being good enough, about being embarrassed and ashamed and generally, feeling thoroughly unhappy and ill at ease in this situation.

She used the rhythm of the music, her body movements and deliberate EMO right there on the dance floor to "dance out" all her pain and misery, and by the time the clock struck midnight, she was glowing, having the time of her life and "was kissed by many more than I've ever experienced before!"

The Energy Of Learning Exercises

When energy flow increases, information flow increases too. This was a surprise, a bonus we didn't expect when we first started to do EMO back in the day; but it soon became apparent that the additional gain in important information is a structural part of improving energy flow in the body.

We certainly noticed how people would say that they felt so much more connected to a person when they had used EMO on their feelings about that person; and there were many fascinating examples that made us think of what happens when energy flow increases in the body in a whole new way, opening the door to all these wonderful new ways of learning from each other and from everything there is, indeed.

Here are three easy EMO exercises to have your own "enlightening" personal experiences with the energy of learning.

Learning From A Favourite Teacher

1. Find a picture of a teacher you admire or a person who inspires you.

2. Pay attention - where do you feel this person in your body? Show it with your hands.

3. If you don't feel anything at all, find the shield - where is the shield? Feel it with your hands.

4. Make a small hole in the shield so that a little of the energy can come in. Now you too are at Step 3: Where do you feel this person in your body? Show yourself with your hands.

5. If healing, unblocking is required, do this now, using your energy hands and the instruction, "Soften and flow."

6. Trace the pathway the energy takes all the way in, through and out.

7. Do any further repair work until the path flows smoothly.

8. Allow the energy to rush fast through your systems until you feel light, delighted, electric, tingling, good, alive.

9. Now take some time to consider what you know now that you didn't know before you started the exercise.

If you wish, make a note of particularly important insights; this might also lead you to another person or a subject about which you might want to learn more, using the energy of learning.

As an additional bonus, you can use the same exercise to learn more from other beings and entities too, such as saints, prophets, angels, deities, and even God itself, should you choose to do so.

Energy, Information & Love

This is a particularly powerful and transformational exercise.

1. Pick some one or some thing you have every reason to hate or dislike so powerfully that you can really feel it in your body.

2. Get a photograph or representation of that which you hate or write a description of it on a piece of paper you can see clearly to help keep your focus in this exercise.

3. Face that which you hate and ask yourself, "Where do I feel that in my body?" Show yourself with your hands.

4. If you have shields against this incoming energy, make a tiny hole in it so you can "taste" the energy and how it feels in your body; then you too are ready for the next step.

5. Use your hands of energy and your intention on the erea you have found and support the process with saying and thinking, "Soften and flow, this is only an energy."

6. Breathe and move your body to encourage the energy flow as it starts to move.

7. If the experience of the moving energy feels unpleasant, soften the energy more until it flows smoothly in, through and out.

8. Using the focal representation, work with that energy until it flows quickly and smoothly, then really fast until it feels tingly, electric, alive and wide awake.

9. Now, consider that which is the focus - what has changed in the way you feel? What has changed in the way you think? What have you learned? And where do you notice the increase in "love"?

This is powerful exercise which represents one of the best challenges in personal development and likewise, can carry the highest rewards.

An EMO trainer from the Middle East used this exercise on a traditional enemy of his people, to test the validity that you can really change "hate to love" by simply working with the energy flow in your body. The very thought of the enemy caused him to experience extreme psychosomatic pain in his chest, in his head, and even in his groin. Just by noticing that he commented that it was no wonder that anything the enemy did or did not do would cause such intense emotional responses in people of his kind; but was brave and went on to treat these ereas which had been discovered until the Even Flow was established and he was in an EMO Energized End State.

There, he expressed an overwhelming compassion for both his own people and the enemy; locked into an impossible struggle that no-one could win as they were. He also said that he felt strongly that trying to seek "peace" or these two groups ignoring each other wasn't the answer at all - that in order to overcome all these millennia of pain and war, they needed to somehow have good transformational experiences with each other, a celebration of some kind that involved them both. Of course he knew that this was not likely to be happening any time soon, but it deeply changed the way he thought and felt about the entire conflict, and he said afterwards that he was extremely grateful to feel love, compassion and understanding for both sides, and whatever else would come to pass, he felt like a better person because of it.

I was there when this happened and I learned from it that you can't change societies, or races, or countries - you can only change people, one at a time at that. At the same time, we don't have power over other people's hearts and minds, only over our own, and in the end, it is up to each one of us what we do with what we've got.

I'll leave that thought with you.

EMO Magic Book Learning

In this exercise, we are going to consider a book as an energy object.

All objects have energy dimensions, but books are particularly interesting because their energy has a lot to do with who wrote the book, and what it is about. This goes far further than just the difference in the sequence of letters that form the words, the sentences and the paragraphs on the pages; and without that extra dimension of information, books can be rather flat and only 3 dimensional when we could learn so much more.

There are many reports about a famous psychic, Edgar Cayce, who would "sleep with a book under his pillow" and be able to recount the content; this may sound a little advanced from where we stand right now, but even an absolute beginner in the use of their 6th sense can learn to tell the difference between books, even if they're all pretty rectangular and all made from paper and binding.

It's a fascinating exercise, I highly recommend it.

1. Choose three physical books from your book shelf.

2. Pay particular attention to how each one feels different in your body, and how each one is unique in the way the energy flow makes you feel.

3. If you find any blocks, unpleasant sensations or shields, take care of them - it's only energy, soften and flow.

4. Using the basic EMO Energy Nutrition protocol, let the energy of each one flow in, through and out, and until you have reached the EMO Energized End State.

5. What have you learned as a result of this exercise?

This is a great introduction exercise to using the energy of learning in different ways, for example to help choose a book that you will purchase and bring into your home and into your life.

It is also an excellent example of the old adage that you should never judge a book by its cover; and for us EMOrs, to never judge any object by physical appearances alone.

Heart Healing

The EMO Heart Healing exercise came into being when I received a message for help from a lady who had been sexually abused as a child and, now in her mid twenties, wasn't getting any better, but worse instead.

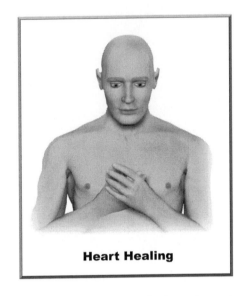

Heart Healing

This often happens to people whose energy systems have been significantly damaged; if this is not healed, the symptoms build up over time, create further problems down the line and things get worse - and time is not healing this.

This particular young lady needed something - but where do you start when all things are in disarray and there's hardly any power left?

I asked myself that question and the Heart Healing poem/prayer came to me; I sent it to her and it helped her become calmer and more stable. I published it later on and so many people found it so very helpful that it became an integral part of EMO and working with energy, especially if a person is suffering from true heartache, a broken heart and other forms of overwhelming emotions.

The "heart of energy" is one of three major systems in the energy body and when we focus our healing intention and healing energy there, the entire system becomes calmer and more stable.

190

Even if a person knows nothing about EMO, the simple Heart Healing exercise is really easy to show and to do, as well as being very effective and beneficial.

1. Place both of your healing hands in the centre of your chest.

2. Take a moment to breathe deeply, in and out, look at your hands and focus on your heart of energy, the powerful nuclear reactor at the centre of your entire energy system.

3. Now think and say the following:

I place my own healing hands
on my own dear heart
to give it all my love
to give it all my support
to give it all I have to give
to heal what was broken
to put to rights
what has gone wrong
to restore the Even Flow
so that my heart of energy
may shine once more
bright and golden
like the sun.

You can use your own words to express the same meaning; the main point here is to channel what you have to give to where it does the most good overall, and that would be to heal, strengthen and support the heart of energy which powers everything else.

For very intense emotional situations, such as immediately after a bereavement or an accident, the onset of a physical illness or intense love pain we now prescribe a course of Heart Healing three times a day for three times three days to provide the essential basic support, plus recommend it for further use as and when it feels needed.

191

The EMO Energy Billionaire

Many spiritual people are always conflicted about "material wealth" and try not to want anything material.

Saying NO to anything is not a good thing in the worlds of energy, and our energy minds, who take everything very literally, might work hard, day and night, to keep any form of material wealth at bay, being very inventive!

Energy flow works best when it is truthful, without contortions of shame, denials, flat out lies, or trying to be better than we really are. All of that makes us worse people because it blocks energy flow. The EMO Energy Billionaire puts an end to this nonsense.

You can be honest about anything material you need, want or positively crave - you just need to put the word "energy" behind it, and it's yours!

For this exercise, pick any material luxury object you are really drawn to. For once, you don't have to explain why, or be ashamed, just pick something you would love to own.

As an example, I'll choose "diamond bracelet energy."

> 1. Where do you feel that diamond bracelet energy in your body? Show me/yourself with your hands.
>
> 2. It's only an energy! Soften and flow!
>
> 3. Trace the channel and soften any blocks until the energy runs freely.
>
> 4. Allow more and more energy to rush in, through and out until you are thoroughly energized!

EMOing the energy of material objects in, through and out whenever and wherever you notice something you desire makes you into the proverbial energy billionaire - it doesn't cost a dime and you're taking nothing away from anyone else :-)

Easy EMO Partner Exercises

All the exercises so far can be done by one person, with a partner or in a group situation.

Here are some examples of EMO experiences that are wonderful to play with a friend or a loved one and which bring out the "client practitioner dance" aspects of doing EMO with another person, even if there are no clients or practitioners, but friends, mother and son, sister and brother or husband and wife present instead.

Call a friend on the phone, try it out, have some fun with energy.

These exercises are also used in the EMO Practitioner Training program to warm up and learn the basics correctly, so I recommend these highly.

The Insult Game

This is the first EMO game that was ever officially played, and it is still one of the best to teach us the basics of how EMO works.

One partner chooses an insult that really hurts them, so much so that they cringe in pain, turn red, get angry or can really feel the physical results of what is "just words" when we don't take the energy worlds into consideration.

If you can't think of anything, think back when you were at school, there are usually lots of insults that were hurled back then, caused pain and which were never properly dealt with.

Once you have the insult, such as, "You have a big nose!" or "You'll never amount to anything!" or "You're a fat pig!" or "You're so stupid!" etc. etc. the owner of the insult trains their partner to say it in the right way.

The partner needs to put some energy into those words, to really mean it and project that energy form of, "You're a fat pig!" with a will to make an impact.

Now, the practitioner partner delivers the insult and watches carefully how the other responds.

Do they flinch back? Move away? What are their hands doing? Their faces? It is very interesting to observe the reaction to an "incoming energy form" that is instant and entirely unconscious.

Now we say, "Where do you feel that in your body? Show me with your hands."

That's really important, even if the hands have already gone to the place of disturbance, we want to say it anyway. Both the client and practitioner in EMO need to know what is happening and it is often very important for the client to "see for themselves that their hands already know."

Once we have the location of the injury or blockage, we say, "This is only an energy, and we can soften and flow that energy."

Say it every time in practice or in play; it is important we both hear it and say it until it becomes second nature to think it when other emotional upsets happen in the real world.

Now we say, "I'm going to help with my intention from the outside, and you help with your intention and your healing hands from the inside, and we are going to soften and flow that energy. Where does that energy need to go?"

If a person doesn't know or can't answer that, just try a few directions. It is easy and instant to know when you're going wrong. For example, "Does it want to move downwards?" will result in an instant, "God no! Oooh that feels awful!" type response if it is wrong. You can try up/down, left/right, in/out until you get the right direction, and we can take it from there.

Every so often, repeat the original insult if you are the practitioner to keep the session on track. Try and keep the energy you send the same each time; even ramp it up and become more intense once the energy starts to flow in the client partner.

Now repeat this and make the flow faster and faster until the person stops suffering and starts laughing.

Look for physical changes - changes in their voice, in how they are sitting and moving; in the colour in their cheeks. All that changes when a person comes to life in the EMO Energized End State and until you can really see, hear and feel the difference, you haven't reached the EMO Energized End State yet and there's more work left to be done.

Sometimes, the energy doesn't move fast enough. There could be something in the system that is slowing it down - where is that in the body? Show me with your hands.

Or the person says that they can't move the energy fast. For some reason, the idea causes them stress - where do they feel that stress in their body? It's fear of what might happen, but if we stick with the word and concept of stress, it's easier for people to deal with and go with the flow.

When you have done such supporting work, it is really important to come back to the original insult, because that is what this session is about, nothing else.

Try not to get side tracked into other issues.

Get the insult done, get it to the EMO Energized End State and then take some time to discuss what happened. Also discuss how it was for the practitioner partner, how they felt, what they felt because that is also important in learning EMO.

Here is another partner exercise which may reveal the presence of shields.

The Praise Game

Pick something that you wish you were but know you're not - such as, "You are beautiful" - "You are intelligent" - "You are a genius" - "You are a wonderful teacher" - "You are so talented" - "You are so young" etc.

Have the practitioner partner take a moment, raise the requisite energy of truth being spoken and then say the words.

Between the two of you, discover how it makes you feel to speak and to receive those words.

Find out if there are shields and have a go at making small holes into them, before running the complete EMO process on this.

It's exciting, powerful and very good fun and both partners learn a lot about each other, about themselves and of course, about EMO.

The Words I've Always Wanted To Hear Game

I observed at one time that the lyrics for music by popular boy and girl bands respectively consist of statements that people desperately want to hear, but which are never ever spoken in any real relationship.

There exists clearly a hunger for such words that people always wanted to hear, but no-one ever says, or at least not to them; so this is a great game to fill an old hunger and learn something new about the power of energy to transform just about every aspect of our human lives right here on Planet Earth.

Take a moment to discuss with your partner what words each one of you always wanted to hear but never did hear, or feel for that matter.

If you are getting worried that this is becoming too intimate, and you might inadvertently fall in love with your friend or practice partner, you might like to EMO that worried sensation in the usual way before you start.

In the process of any EMO practice, of course we are going to gain energy, information and love, but it is clean love - unconditional love that doesn't lead to negative obsessions or weird after-effects.

So when you are ready, and you have a set of words each, have a go at teaching each other how to say the words you've always wanted to hear so they are said right, then EMO what happens next.

Here it is, step by step:

1. Find some words you always longed to hear (but nobody ever said them to you).

2. Coach your partner in saying them to you with meaning and intention. Help your partner overcome any reversals they might be experiencing about this so they can say the words cleanly, and they carry clean and powerful energies.

3. Make them say the words you always wanted to hear.

4. Deal with any shields by allowing a small amount of energy to come in as usual.

5. Now EMO this energy you have longed for all the way in, through and out - don't hold on to it, no matter how good it feels, it isn't healthy, energy needs to flow!

6. Do this until the EMO Energized End State has happened and you are both absolutely delighted, joyous, laughing, energized.

7. Spend some time to discuss with your partner what happened, and how this has changed you.

8. Then swop around - your partner deserves to hear some words they have waited for so long and have this amazing energy experience too!

I had an interesting experience with this exercise which I set for a group in German EMO Training. There was a lady who was - well, let's say not the easiest person to get on with. She was constantly complaining and just before this session had started, I had observed her holding up the entire dining room with her complaints and being very rude to the poor girl at the payment desk.

I set the exercise, made my rounds and noted her with her partner. I asked what the words where this lady always wanted to hear, and she said, "You are such a wonderful person." I must admit, that blew my mind for a moment; it also had the same effect on her practice partner. I watched the two go to work with great interest;

the difficult lady continued to be difficult; the practice partner did their best and succeeded eventually in getting the huge blocks in her stomach, chest and throat to shift and flow away. The lady transformed, cried, smiled, hugged her partner and I kept an eye on her for the rest of the training - she never complained once again, not to us, not in the venue, not about anything and by the end, people really liked her and like working with her.

To this day I'm amazed at the transformation, and how those very words this lady always needed to hear were the key, so perfectly, to set her free to be herself - a really kind, lovely lady who had so much to give.

This is an extraordinary, powerful and very educational experience that has as an interesting long term side effect - you get to understand how it works, and when the situation arises, you can actually say to a person the words they always wanted to hear but no-one ever spoke them. This is a gift much beyond just being a core skill for lovers, parents and teachers to understand and get very good at doing.

The Relationship Game

There are many possible versions of this that can be employed for relationship counselling in different ways; by for example dealing with something that has upset one of the partners, whatever it may be, finding the location and healing that to the EMO Energized End State when energy, information and love transform the entire experience.

We can say what upsets us but we can also simply deal with something without naming it; therefore we can ask in a couple session, "Where do you have something that is causing trouble in the relationship, where do you feel it in your body, show me with your hands," and thus avoid "upsetting" anyone even further.

Regardless of whether what causes problems in the relationship is profound jealousy or just being annoyed daily that the toothpaste cap is being left off, "it is only an energy" and we can bring back the Even Flow to this aspect of the relationship easily. When both partners are encouraged to work with and on each other, and engage in the client practitioner dance together, wonderful things happen in relationships.

This particular game works as follows.

1. Look at your partner.

2. Identify something that irritates or annoy you about them, or something that gets in the way of having a better relationship. You can think in terms of a quality such as, "he's lazy," or "he's inconsiderate" or in terms of a specific memory, "I'll never forgive him for forgetting my birthday last year, it broke my heart" or perhaps a judgement such as, "I really don't like his views on politics," or a judgement on the physical appearance, "I wish he'd get a haircut."

3. Make sure you can feel a strong emotional reaction, something you can really feel in your body.

4. Where do you feel this in your body? Show us with your hands.

5. Now let your partner help you move the energy, soften and flow until it flows in, through and out.

6. Look at your partner again and re-call the original problem. Make sure not a trace remains and all flows fast and smoothly in, through and out.

7. Switch over.

8. When both partners have reached the EMO Energized End State, tell each other how you feel about each other now. Describe what your really feel in your body, don't say, "I love you," but use Lucian's language instead - "I feel a huge, huge warmth coming from the centre of my chest when I look at you." Priceless.

Apart from the many applications this has in direct partner work, you can also do this by yourself with a photograph of your partner to take out "daily rubbish" that accumulates in the energy system, especially in long term relationships, to keep things fresh, bright, young, and always, always new and exciting.

Daily Energy Awareness Exercises

EMO is all about becoming aware of our 6th sense that expresses itself through felt sensations in the body we call our emotions.

Energy awareness literally transforms our lives for the better. It shows us what needs healing and how to heal that; it allows us to have wonderful experiences and have these under our own control, and any time we choose to tap into the oceans of energy with volition.

Energy is the missing X-factor is so many equations that don't make any sense until and unless you take the energy worlds into consideration, and then they do - the world becomes logical, we become more logical and more effective as a direct result.

The world becomes less confusing, less fear filled and our stress recedes; the less stressed we are, the easier it is to be happy, to make good decisions and to have an open mind that thinks clearly and comes up with inspirational solutions to old problems, too.

So here are some simple and easy daily exercises to consider; when we start to pay attention to energy movements, energy occurrences and how they manifest in our lives, we gain more energy, more love and more information in turn. The more we practice this, the better it gets, without any upward limit that I can perceive.

When you have energy awareness, life becomes wonderful, so I recommend these exercises particularly to you.

Pay With Attention, Gain More Energy Awareness

Start to actively pay attention to energy manifestations you can feel in your own body.

Pay attention to your own body feelings.

Take a moment every so often to notice how you feel. Pay attention to physical sensations, such as the feel of your feet on the ground, the fit of your clothes, the feel of the air on your hands, in your hair.

Then pay attention to your sensations - how do you feel inside? Are there any parts of you that feel unhappy, tight, tense? Could a little movement and movement of energy, a little "Soften & Flow" improve how you feel right now?

Do this often; these small regular practice sessions in energy movements and energy awareness are the key to the "big movements" when they come.

Pay attention to your body movements and hand gestures, and those of other people.

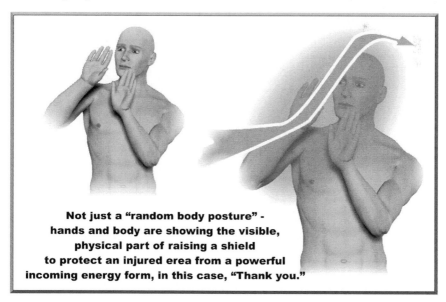

Not just a "random body posture" -
hands and body are showing the visible,
physical part of raising a shield
to protect an injured erea from a powerful
incoming energy form, in this case, "Thank you."

203

Pay attention to where people put their hands on their own bodies when they talk about their problems or their daily tasks. Even when you are watching TV, pay attention to how people react when they are in emotional pain, or if they have been shocked, or when they show you where their shields are with their hands.

Even though energy is invisible in and of itself, you can really see the places where it happens and is being described by people.

Listen to what people say when they talk about their emotions and feelings. The words we use are not random and when someone says, "I feel deflated," or "I feel so depressed ..." learn to link that up with the conditions in their energy systems which are perfectly real and not just in their minds.

Most importantly, pay attention to your own emotions and feelings. They are happening all the time, frustrations rising, laughter bubbling up, a wave of sadness sweeping over you, pressure building up - your own body and your own experiences in response to life as it happens is your best trainer in energy awareness.

Once you start to pay attention, you will be able to pick up the influences and results of the invisible energy movements in us and around us which are happening all the time, a real widening of horizons and a real forward movement in energy awareness.

"It's Only An Energy!" Exercise

When you feel emotions, say to yourself, "This is only an energy ..." and notice how this affects the way your mind and your body responds to that message.

Most of the time, you can feel a softening beginning to occur already, right there and then.

You can support this by focusing on where you feel your emotion, touch there with your healing hands of energy and by thinking, "That's right, soften and flow ..."

Even if you don't always immediately reach the EMO Energized End State, each time you do this, you are improving your ability to understand and cope with emotions in a whole new way.

In this context, it is also interesting to take some time to sit down and wonder what your life might be like if you were never again afraid of certain things that in the past caused you to experience emotional pain when you tried to do them.

Conversely, when you have a person in your environment who is having an emotional disturbance, be it a child who throws a screaming fit tantrum or an adult who is angry, sad or depressed, take a moment to think to yourself, "This is only an energy."

You might not be able to say that to a person who doesn't know EMO, but notice how you knowing that and recognising that for what it is, someone reacting to a condition in their energy body and nothing more, changes YOUR feelings towards the entire situation.

Learning to think of all human emotions and their varied expressions in terms of this being structural, systemic and "only an energy" really helps to be more patient, more compassionate, more loving and more logical in how to deal with that.

Developing Your 6th Sense

EMO has demonstrated to us that we have six senses - feeling, seeing, hearing, scenting, tasting and the 6th sense, which is sensing the energy dimensions.

When all six senses are working together, we gain more information about anything we are paying attention to, and that includes warnings about negative influences in the environment that could save your life.

These warnings, known as "intuitions," are the same system as our emotions, the non-physical sensations, and we get better at working with our sixth sense through the daily practice of EMO.

We can practice this in many ways, all of which are fascinating and serve to illustrate how our sixth sense can give us additional information about the invisible worlds of energy we can feel in our own bodies.

As a simple example, you can stand in a book shop and choose a book not by what it looks like but what it feels like when you feel it in your body.

That is the basic, simple EMO protocol - where do I feel this in my body? Show me with my hands. Have an energy experience and use what you have learned (the energy of learning) to guide you which book to buy and which to leave on the shelf.

The same can be done with many different things, choosing the right item from a restaurant menu, for example, or one type of fruit from a selection in a supermarket isle.

I did this once whilst on holiday in France and got a strong negative physical response to the mussel soup as I was reading the menu. Just reading it made me feel very nauseous but it was only that one item. I warned my dinner companions against ordering it. Two of them ignored my advice and got sick with food poisoning.

206

Afterwards, everyone declared me to be psychic; I like to think of using my God given 6th sense for exactly what it was designed for in the first place, to tell me what is good to eat, and what isn't, even if we can't see, hear, taste or smell the difference.

Any energy based interaction with any object - Where do I feel this in my body? Show me with my hands! - will give you *additional information* about that object which, as in the case of the mussel soup, can be potentially beneficial, even life saving.

When it comes to decision making, I hold that those who make decisions without consulting the additional information our 6th sense can provide us with do so at their own peril.

People Energy Practice

"Where do I feel this person in my body? Show me with my hands!" is a fascinating doorway to learning a lot about our own shields and injuries, blockages and reversals and often the reasons for why we don't get on with certain people, or in certain situations.

To deal successfully with people, and these are all unique, individual people, the ground rule is that the smoother their energy can flow into you, through you and out, the more you know about them, and the safer you are from them, too.

The additional energy information you gain through your sixth sense is more truthful and direct than what is being show to you, or what is being said.

Without shields or negative reactions due to previous energy injuries from that type of person, the reactions of people to you become entirely different as well.

One of the first ever EMO sessions involved a lady who was being stalked and had entirely cocooned herself from that aggressive energy; the more she shielded herself, the worse the stalker had become.

When she let a tiny bit of the stalker's energy into her body, through the smallest laser pin prick hole near her left little finger, this energy went "into her bones and strengthened her bones" - leading to a threshold shift which, amongst other things, included the memory of her father calling her "spineless" after she failed to stand up to him.

"As if by magic" the stalker ceased stalking shortly after the EMO session had been done and the lady had felt strong and powerful and had dropped her shield.

There is no magic in that unless you want to call it energy magic; this outcome is a natural, normal, direct energy based response. While her energy system had been "spineless" and weak, the stalker sensed her as a target; when it changed, she and her energy became unattractive to the stalker and he went away to find someone else who was weak instead.

Don't be afraid to repair injuries from people in the past and take in the energy of similar people now - more energy is always strengthening, empowering, and you get more information and more love as well and free of charge.

EMO By Proxy

This is an excellent exercise in pure energy experience - instead of working with your own energy sensations, you work with someone else's energy through EMO by proxy.

Instead of saying, "Where do I feel my anger in my body?" we ask, "Where do I feel Peter's anger in my body? Show me with my hands."

When we move Peter's energy through our own bodies, many interesting things happen.

Firstly, we understand Peter's "anger" much better - that is the bonus of the additional information.

Secondly, we feel much closer to Peter - that is the bonus of additional love.

The third effect is that Peter changes.

Energy work is non-local, non-temporal, and we really are all connected at the energy levels and in the energy dimensions.

Once you get more comfortable navigating the oceans of energy, you will understand how it work in that personal, experiential way and you probably won't until you do.

You can do EMO by proxy on your loved ones, here, near and far; you can do it on animals, which is very telling, because animals can't pretend to have changed just to do me a favour and support my theories.

Actively look for opportunities to use this to your advantage and to change people in the energy way.

For example, "Where do I feel my husbands inability to communicate in MY body? Show me with my hands!" can be useful; and, "Where do I feel my boss being stressed out of his mind in my body? Show me with my hands!"

I can even attest to using this on a traffic cop who stopped me, with a silent, "Where do I feel this man's suspicion in my body? Soften and flow ..." upon which he quite "miraculously" started to smile, gave me my licence back and waved me on my way.

The Mirror Man Exercise

This is a simple daily energy awareness exercise which I particularly treasure.

When we get up in the mornings, we go into the bathroom to wash up and brush our teeth. In the course of this, of course we look into the mirror and meet the mirror man.

Stop for a moment and look into the mirror man's eyes.

Where do you feel that person in your body this morning?

Take a deep breath, soften and flow.

As your energy builds up, so does the mirror man's energy in reflection; continue until you are quite in love and there are no shields and no judgements left, only energy, information and love.

Do this exercise every morning and every night and you will transform your incarnation even if you never do anything else, and that is guaranteed.

PART 4 - EMO A-Z

EMO And ...

The structural simplicity of EMO in theory and practice makes it applicable to every human problem that involves any kind of emotion (and can you think of a single human problem that does not involve emotions?).

As long as you can stick to the basic precepts and don't stray from the elegance and simplicity of basic EMO, it may be applied to literally everything.

This includes the obvious relationship problems, self concept and self identity problems, emotional injuries sustained through bereavement, trauma, abuse, physical illness and accident; emotional relationships to substances and objects such as allergies, fetishes and addictions; the healing of psychosomatic pains and phantom pains; but it also includes performance enhancement across the board.

When energy flow is smooth and lively, there isn't a thing that people do that they can't do eve better still when energy flow improves even further.

Whether it is golf, physical fitness, chess or public speaking, singing, painting, overcoming writer's block, becoming a more powerful healer or singer, developing your X factor and personal charisma, improving the experience of your spiritual practice or simply seeking powerful inspiration in any area or any topic matter, when you work with EMO, we have a wonderful tool to really transform the emotional experience of anything at all.

More energy, more information, more love - we deserve more and with EMO, we can have more, right now!

There is another strand to how the structural simplicity and the pure focus on energy work of EMO can help across the board.

EMO can be added to many other existing modalities of human healing, personal development and evolution to bring in that extra energy awareness, that extra energy dimension, and it makes what is already good even better in the process.

- Adding basic EMO to a massage for example entirely transforms the experience for the masseur as well as for their client;

- Adding EMO to Aromatherapy unlocks a whole new level of wonderful energy experiences that bring the body, mind and spirit back to life;

- EMO combines easily and beautifully with Reiki. In fact, the much dreaded "healing crisis" in Reiki can be entirely avoided by working with EMO to help clear the channels, and of course, it allows the practitioner to flow massively more energy without hurting themselves in the process.

- EMO powers EFT to a whole new level in energy awareness, finding the right set ups, encouraging energy flow and getting a real +10 Healing Event at the end;

- EMO gives logic and meaning to NLP by adding the 6th sense and finally defining the mysterious "deep structure" which NLP interventions seek to change;

- EMO empowers all forms of metaphor work and including Project Sanctuary once it has been learned and understood because reading the energy behind the metaphor and dealing with it appropriately can only be done with a well developed 6th sense;

- EMO is perfect to use with Events Psychology and because of its structure, can be used within talking therapy environments and other healing environments where energy work is normally not accepted or would be frowned upon.

EMO can make many things a lot easier for both the practitioner as well as for the client; and when you combine EMO with kinesiology, meditation, body work, yoga, Tai Chi, Karate, Kung Fu, physical therapy or any other type of human change work, you will find it smooths the flow of the session and speeds up the results than can be achieved dramatically and without getting in the way of the process.

The following short examples are here to give you ideas on where and how you can use EMO to improve our experiences with our own bodies, our feelings and emotions, our intellectual capacity to understand ourselves, other people and the world at large, and our capacity to love and feel loved in return.

EMO and The 6th Sense

The practice of EMO over the past decade has taught us that the 6th sense is indeed the sensations in the body which are created by non-physical information.

This is the important additional information that, which added to the information from the other 5 senses, creates the experience of reading and understanding a field of information which is as good as it can get for a human being at our level of development.

Information about energy is more important than people realise.

First of all, without an awareness of energy exchanges between people and their world, very little makes sense, and much less feels good. Without the addition of the energy worlds and how humans respond through that with the medium of their emotions, the world is indeed a hard place, a dark place, a place without hope, without love, and filled with the terror of loneliness and death.

Living in such a world, being blind to energy isn't just a tragedy; from this blind place of darkness, further unfortunate choices and decisions are made that are not natural to human beings at all. Patterns and strategies are used that are counterproductive and make an already bad situation even worse.

Energy awareness, our 6th sense that we all possess, is the key to many things. With energy awareness, we can make better choices based on more information. We have it in our own hands, metaphorically speaking and here being the representatives of our whole bodies, to choose to feel better, to learn more, to love more. Our 6th sense of energy awareness understands flow and how all things are connected; and it can warn us when natural laws are being contravened so we do not need to descend into the chaos that follows as surely as day follows night.

With the 6th sense functioning as it should, we can become aware of betrayal and attempts at lies and deceit; if we hone our 6th sense

218

enough, we can read so much off the energy systems of other people that it seems we have become empathic, telepathic, clairvoyant.

Coupled with the human consciousness, which can move freely amidst space and time at will, we have information past, present and future that can be read like the proverbial book when the 6th sense is fully operational and we have learned to understand how to read and process that additional information the energy worlds provide.

EMO is a simple step, a baby step, to bring us back to the reality of the 6th sense. We can feel it through our bodies; there is an enormous dictionary of sensations and their correlated informational meanings awaiting those who start on that very first step, which is to become aware of massive emotional disturbances, a self diagnostic system which has been uncoupled, forgotten and entirely misunderstood until now.

From the massive emotional disturbances, and how it feels when these begin to soften and flow, how that changes our emotions, our energy levels and our cognition, we begin to learn the real first brightly coloured lessons of our own 6th senses.

After that, we become more energy aware.

This is extremely important, because we pay with attention and we gain energy, information and love in return. When we pay attention to other people's shields, and consciously notice that when someone paints them into the air with their hands for all to see, we are taking one step further into activating our 6th sense, using it, bringing it online.

Every time you feel a stress response, or an emotion; a fleeting sensation like a shiver in a warm room, a little tightness in the back of the neck upon entering a building; every time we notice this, pay attention and think to ourselves, "Ah, an energy occurrence ..." our experience begins to grow and we begin to understand ourselves a little better.

Then we move on to using the energy of learning to help us discover beneficial food to eat from a choice of many different items; to resolve shields and blockages to incoming energy forms. In doing so, we are literally repairing the pathways that belong to the 6th sense and restoring our ability to read more and more information from the environment at large.

In the past it has been so that people have been divided into those who are good at hearing, and they became musicians. Those who were good at seeing, became watchers. Those who were good with their bodies became soldiers and sports people. Those who were good with taste became cooks, and those who were good with scent, became aromatherapists. Those who were good with reading energetic realities were made into witches or priests, depending on where you find yourself in space and time.

The fact is to be a fully functional human being who lives life according to their own creative template and as the Creative Order designed us to be, we need to make use of all of our senses.

If you have a favourite sense, consider it not to be the one and only saviour of your incarnation, consider it an entry point into the world of the six senses and strive to build up the others so they get just as good as the first and favourite sense.

Paying attention to the energy worlds also unlocks our other senses as a bye the bye. When energy blockages, pain, misery and depression are being replaced with Even Flow, joy and EMO Energized End States, people comment that the lights are so much brighter, the colours so much richer, food tastes so much better, scents are so amazing that you nearly faint and sounds become a wondrous tapestry.

The 6th sense isn't a spooky something for the chosen few to practice when darkness falls; EMO proves to us that it is your birthright to know it, to understand it, and most of all to use it to navigate reality absolute in safety and confidence, so you can have the best possible experiences in your life this life has to offer.

220

EMO and Addictions

There has never been anything like EMO to help a person who is struggling with addiction to address the very real feelings in their body - the powerful waves of needing and hunger, the stress and fear associated with the addiction, the pains of withdrawal, to mention but a few.

All of these can be significantly alleviated with EMO.

But there is more.

The underlying emotional reasons for the addiction and the negative emotions the addictive substance has alleviated in the past can also be addressed with EMO. The first and most obvious energy injuries can be treated with the help of a practitioner and there, the person learns how to use EMO in self healing. They can take this away and treat themselves for all and any emotions that arise in daily life right there and then, which is where the healing is needed the most.

There is a third unique aspect in working with EMO and addictions, and that is by working with the energetic relationships between the person and the addictive substance, action or object.

Often, the relationship starts with a powerful positive emotional experience of joy, pain relieved, peace having been experienced; this is called a Guiding Star which is the opposite of a trauma. When there is a powerful positive emotional experience, it becomes very difficult for a person to stop seeking to have that experience again, even if it never works again, and even if that quest for the experience results in life damaging or even life threatening behaviours.

With EMO, we can address and evolve those strong positive feelings that the substance, behaviour or object evoked and thus free people from the Guiding Star experience.

This is of the essence in all work with addictions and without addressing the positive emotional experiences that underlie the energetic relationship between a person and their addiction, it is

221

either immensely difficult or simply impossible to create a movement towards being free of that substance.

A fourth additional benefit of addressing addictions with EMO is the additional possibilities of energy nutrition. With EMO, many things can be used to create powerful positive emotions, such as deliberately drawing in the energy of a sunrise, an ocean or the starry night; animals and people too. For many people with addictions, to have something else that can alleviate stress profoundly and make them feel good, better even than the old addictive Guiding Star, is the turning point away from the addiction, and towards a future where the world itself provides powerful positive emotional experiences but for the asking.

EMO and Anger

Anger and rage are human emotions that are not easily "managed" in the conventional sense. When we take them as energy occurrences, we can take a different point of view.

Firstly, basic EMO theory holds that there are no good energies or bad energies; there's only energy. If it feels bad, that's because of a blockage or a reversal.

Anger doesn't feel bad - at least not at the time. It is a powerful energy movement that can be very, very fast indeed and the effects on the entire mind, body, energy body system are truly profound as anyone can attest to who has seen someone "turn" from a fairly ordinary person into a truly scary rage monster in an instance.

It is frightening; and never more frightening than for the person who lives that, has to live with that and experience the results and repercussions after the fact when there was nothing they could have done differently, given the circumstances and their unique set ups.

People who experience extreme rage and anger when it is triggered are terrified of themselves above all else; and that's the first place to start with the EMO intervention.

"Do you scare yourself? Where do you feel that in your body?"

Through experience we have learned that people who have uncontrollable anger outbursts have tried their hardest in the past to stay patient, to not get angry - but without the energy paradigm, that's impossible and so there is a lot of failure, guilt and shame and anger at the self built up over time. All these things are also however only an energy, and to tell someone who has been suffering from this particular affliction all their lives is a huge blessing, a benediction.

As with all extreme emotional problems, once we have dealt with the first and most obvious ereas that need attention, it is important

223

to make the person aware of how they feel stress and where they feel that in their body.

An anger explosion is literally that - an explosion caused by too much stress on the system, and something has to give. To understand general stress build up is very important in the treatment of anger and rage related energy injuries; but it's not the answer, for anger comes from out of nowhere, like a lightning strike and without any previous warnings on occasion.

This is why people who have anger problems are constantly on guard, terrified of letting their guard down and hurting an innocent bystander against their will. Yet letting their guard down, read releasing a shield or more than one, is an important part of the healing process with EMO.

Here is one very interesting observation that you might like to share with someone who suffers from anger problems, namely that the energy movement itself isn't the problem, and even though it seems so fast, it is actually still too slow.

Imagine if you had that anger flash and it went in, through and out smoothly in less than 1/100th of a second, leaving you tingling, bright and clear, wide awake, wide aware and in an EMO Energized End State.

This is the correct usage of that system that converts into anger when there are injuries and blockages about - it is a wake up call to action, an instant energizing sensation that prepares a person in mind, body and spirit for fight or flight, should this become necessary.

Indeed, you can have any emotion you like - as long as it is a flash that travels smoothly in, through and out, doesn't get stuck anywhere, doesn't explode in an inappropriate place in our network of energy channels, it will always leave you in an EMO Energized End State and feeling wonderful.

Practising with people who have anger problems to move that energy through and out instantly is the answer to anger problems and other types of flash emotions. That's the exact opposite movement from clamping down reflexively and trying to keep the anger down.

This is entirely doable and what it shows is that these anger flashes have their uses in the system - if they are quick, and if they are allowed to produce the EMO Energized End State they are designed to produce naturally, as an important natural survival mechanism. By keeping the original energy movement and its purpose intact, and in fact, furthering that purpose, people can be motivated to learn how to really handle their anger flashes correctly who would otherwise be very resistant, because they know that these powerful explosions got them out of trouble on some occasions, and often even saved their lives.

This understanding how anger works as an energy in the energy system can also help people who are terrified of ever getting angry and have locked down the entire anger system, thereby making themselves weak, defenceless in moments of high crisis, and robbing themselves of a powerful function of a normal energy body.

I would like to point out once more that the lightning strikes we call anger, if they run smoothly through and out, also carry tremendous amounts of information that can be essential to know in survival situations as well as the extra energy required to act at the very top range of an individual's capabilities; but also, there is the third component of these energy streams, which is that of love.

The EMO Energized End State following a fully expressed and "perfectly executed" anger flash contains extreme compassion for all who are present and including the person themselves; it is a powerful, self concept changing event for the energy system so it is well worth practising, whether you have anger "management" problems or not.

EMO and Animals

The very origins of EMO go back to working with relationships between animals and people, the original research on the causes and cures for Attention Seeking Behaviour Disorders.

It was during that research that we found out about the reality of energy exchanges between social mammals, and that when an animal seeks attention, it seeks nourishment that it needs for system survival.

Attention malnutrition leads directly to disturbed behaviours, such as rage syndrome, and conversely, all manner of disturbed behaviour can be cured simply by giving more attention.

This holds true for all social mammals and including people.

When we learn to do EMO, we learn to give more attention in more focused way; being aware of how energy exchanges work, and how people and animals in our environment "ask" for an input of energy through their various attention seeking behaviours is essential information.

In energy exchanges, "a stitch in time saves nine" most profoundly.

When a little bit of focused, positive attention is given instantly when it is asked for, attention seeking behaviour doesn't need to escalate into temper tantrums and much happier relationships result, with much less stress being experienced all around.

Understanding even a little bit about the nature of energy exchanges, and the importance of energy nutrition transforms relationships.

In working and living with animals, such as horse riding and dog and cat ownership, we have daily opportunities to practice good energy practices, such as paying attention when it is asked for, becoming aware of the effects of our emotions which are only energy shifts, and theirs; how we respond to their energy shifts and the behaviours that arise, and how they respond to ours.

Even stroking an animal with the healing hands of energy switched on completely changes the experience for both and results in better relationships.

A very powerful way of working with temperamental or behaviour problems in animals is to use EMO by proxy - "Where do I feel this dog's nervousness in my body?"

This is also extremely interesting, because the feedback you are getting directly through changes in the animal's behaviour is such powerful evidence to the absolute reality of energy and the effects that energy movements have on all of us, for animals can't lie.

Working with the energy exchanges in the relationships with animals is a marvellous thing, and this doesn't end with companion animals and close personal relationships.

A wonderful way of gaining extra energy nutrition (and the requisite extra information, and extra love!) is to open oneself up to the energy of all kinds of animals, including wild animals.

For shamanic practitioners, to really be able to let the energy of a totem animal flow in, through and out and experience a full EMO Energized End State with that animal's energy is a fantastic experience; but anyone who is drawn to a particular species of animals can enrich themselves powerfully by using basic EMO to improve the energy flow between you.

It is my observation that people are drawn to a particular type of animal because this animal contains essential energy nutrients and vitamins that are lacking in a person's systems, so to follow your fascinations with animals and flow their energy forms through you is very healthy for the energy body indeed.

People who have phobias or lower level dislikes against different kinds of animals experience not just relief from negative feelings of terror, fear or dislike, but also find that these dislikes were a diagnostic mechanism to show them where there was something wrong in their energy bodies.

Whenever you become aware of an animal and you have a negative or a positive reaction, do some EMO to the EMO Energized End State; it's excellent stimulation and nutrition for your energy body.

Finally, I'd like to make the comment that understanding how energy works in the human body finally puts an end to the idea that people shouldn't suffer from extreme bereavement upon the death of a beloved companion animal and that such intense bereavement pain should be reserved for members of one's own species alone.

As we are strictly dealing with energy disturbances, I can guarantee for any pet owner who seeks an EMO Master Practitioner to help them with the pain of animal bereavement, they will be treated respectfully, listened to properly and helped in love and without prejudice.

Pain is pain; and we are here to help transform people's experiences from pain to joy, so when there is any type of animal bereavement, think EMO, it's the right way to go.

EMO and Anxiety & Stress

If we consider stress in energetic terms, I think of it like a system that is trying to go fast but it is out of balance, so it starts to vibrate, then shake, and it can literally shake itself apart if the stress becomes too high and goes out of control. This is the progression from stress to anxiety and culminating in the panic attacks at the high end.

When we work with energy and energy awareness, how we feel the workings of our energy system through our physical bodies, we become much more aware of stress as it happens and as it builds up throughout the day.

This is a good thing because stress awareness is the first step to being able to stop and do something about it.

With all forms of stress in general, but especially when stress build up has become so great over time that a person now experiences anxiety attacks and panic attacks, it is of the essence to not just deal with the big stuff, but also to monitor stress levels throughout the day and learn how to respond to the warning signs as early on as possible.

A little EMO energy work to de-stress the energy body and make it feel strong and alive again throughout the day and at the right time often prevents the need for "massive" healing sessions once a month or when a breakdown has occurred.

Here are some tips for stress and anxiety.

- It is well worth it to take a couple of EMO sessions with an experienced energist to make sure you've got the basics right and you understand how to do EMO. During those sessions you can deal with your main problem ereas; there are usually only two or three places in the energy body that are the most damaged or susceptible to stress and once these are working better, you feel better all over, too.

- For self help, before you go to sleep at night, take a moment to consider what stresses you the most right now, find the location in your body and soften and flow until you feel clear and loving again. Going into the night happily leads to better, deeper sleep which you need to wake up refreshed and ready to go the next day.

- When you first wake up, and there is something in the day ahead that immediately causes a spike in your stress levels (something you dread, something you are not looking forward to), take a moment to focus on the body sensations and release the stress energy, finding the pathway it needs to move through your body and out. Repeat this until you feel good and what was previously fearful is something else entirely.

- As your day progresses, stop every so often, at least once an hour, and run the "fast EMO Stress Release Technique" (in the Exercises section) to release any stress that has built up.

- When your stress levels spike into the red, such as a "bad" letter or email, a "bad" phone call, "bad news" on the TV, getting angry or frustrated, stop. Locate the body sensation, show yourself with your hands where it hurts and remind yourself that this is only an energy, take a deep breath then give the instruction to soften and flow. With very bad news or high stress situations, do this often.

The more severe the symptoms of stress and anxiety are in a person, the more important it becomes to really stick to the basic EMO protocol of:

Where do I feel this in my body?
Show me with my hands.
This is only an energy!
Soften and flow!

Do this exactly like that, all four steps, every time, and until the conscious counting out of the steps as you learn to waltz - one, two, three, one, two three - becomes a smooth, flowing dance to the music.

Even if at first it seems a lot of effort to take 2 minutes out to actively de-stress, you will find that with a little bit of practice, the EMO energy release process becomes faster, more profound, and often, you only have to think, "This is only an energy! Soften and flow!" and the energy flow starts up immediately.

Over a period of time you will find that the process kicks in automatically in direct response to stressors in the environment; look forward to that because that is truly awesome and changes your life and the way you think about yourself altogether.

- *To find an EMO Master Practitioner, go to GoE.ac*

EMO and Affirmations

Affirmations are statements of intent, how we want things to be. Affirmations are stated in the first person and in present tense; so a poor person may affirm, "I am rich," a fat person may affirm, "I am thin," and a sick person may affirm, "I am healthy."

The problem with affirmations is that there are usually reasons for why the poor person is poor, the fat person is fat and the sick person is sick; and if these reasons are situated in the energy body in the form of injuries, the energy runs into those blockages which only causes further pain.

As with so many things, when you add EMO into the mix, it starts to work better or for the first time ever; so here is how to do affirmations that work like a charm with EMO.

1. State your affirmation - for this example, let's use the famous old, "Gr, Gr, I'm a tiger!" the executive tries in the bathroom mirror before entering a difficult meeting.

2. Try your best to raise that tiger energy - where do you feel that in your body? Show yourself with your hands.

3. Work on that erea with your energy hands until you can start it to soften and the energy begin to flow.

4. Repeat the affirmation, "I'm a tiger!" and move the energy through fast, encouraging it all the way in, through and out and dissolving any blockages along the way.

5. When the pathway is complete, re-state the affirmation, "I'm a tiger!" and let that energy swish through you fast and until your reach the EMO Energized End State.

6. Enjoy! and reflect upon the fact that you can now make ANY affirmation really work wonders for you - thanks to EMO. This is a priceless gift. How are you going to use it?

EMO and Aromatherapy

Aromatherapy becomes a whole new experience when you add the extra dimension of working with the concentrated energies of essential oils.

Essential oils have their unique and distinctive scents. This engages one of our six senses, one that we use little yet is particularly powerful because it is our oldest and most primal sense, the sense of smell. When we add our sixth sense of energy to the experience, we can notice how essential oils affect our energy body in unique and very precise ways.

As a first EMO aromatherapy experience, simply take a bottle of essential oil and hold it to your heart. Where do you feel the energy of this in your body? Let it flow in, through and out - that creates amazing sensations, different for each different essential oil.

A second wonderful experience is to open the bottle, scent the oil and now track the path of the scent and the energy it brings into your body all the way as it travels not just into your nose and head, but is actually transported all over your body so you can feel it everywhere.

With the addition of EMO, you can learn to match the right essential oil to lift you in all manner of different emotional states, and provide very powerful energy nutrition for all sorts of challenges in daily life and wherever you go.

If you adore Aromatherapy already, adding the EMO energy experiences will unlock a whole new level of joy for you; and if never really "got" what Aromatherapy is all about, with EMO I think you will find why people rave about it. A truly excellent partnership - Highly recommended!

- *See also "Aromatherapy For Your Soul" by Silvia Hartmann, DragonRising 2007*

233

EMO and Art

Art and EMO are an enormously wide ranging and important topic with profound implications for human creativity, innovation and evolution. For many people who have come across EMO and energy nutrition, it has shown them the way towards how to understand, appreciate and connect with art for the first time; this holds true for all art modalities from music across the board, classical and modern art and sculpture, opera to hip hop, ballet to tribal dance and much more besides.

Indeed, without the sixth sense and the awareness of the energy of any work of art, any appreciation of art is relegated to observable craftsmanship which is flat and lifeless in comparison.

One cannot appreciate a work of art without the additional information at the energetic level; many works of art make no sense at all without that, but when you include the additional 6th sense information of "Where do you feel this painting in your body?" and then go on to remove blockages, injuries and barriers to the smooth inflow, through flow and outflow of energy, much more than just that one painting starts to make sense.

A visit to an art gallery becomes a powerful exercise in learning to read energetic realities and once the worst blockages in the energy system that would lead to an instant rejection are out of the way, even with works of art from the same artist, very subtle informational difference become apparent.

A visit to a music event can become transformational when one makes the conscious choice to drop shields, heal any existing blocks and injuries and add the experience of the energy of music flowing without hindrance, in, through and out, and allowing it to change us in the light of the new experience.

We can do so much to re-connect with the true nature of the human spirit when we choose to stop rejecting forms of art that we might have been entrained to find painful, find the courage to understand

234

more, to gain more energy, information and love from the experience.

Apart from gaining all important magic moments, true life events, the power of energy experiences to teach us how to learn is so essential as well.

A Western lady tells the story of attending a tribal ceremony whilst on holiday, opening herself to the experience which included removing stuck energy in her ears and in her lower abdomen. She went to speak to the dancers afterwards because she was so moved and delighted, she wanted to thank them for their wonderful performance. Here it turned out that she had understood what the dance was all about, something that was never told to the tourists, and the dancers declared her to be a shaman - she had to be, how else could she have known?

Learning from the energy inherent in the art of others of our own species across space and time is one thing, and a wonderful thing indeed; when it comes to creating our own messages to give to others, creating our own unique works of art then how essential does the understanding and knowledge of energy become?

EMO has created a complete body of work on modern Energy Art in the form of Art Solutions - how to create works of art in any modality of human expression where the energy is the message and the modality the container that brings form and function together to become one and the same.

For any true artist, and any true human being who longs to be an artist, EMO can and does open the door to an entirely new realm of artistic experiences, artistic manifestations and leaving a legacy of information that others might come across in the future or the present, read back and understand.

- *Further information: EnergyArt.uk - Energy Art, Primal Art, Art Solutions*

EMO and Artefacts

Artefacts are objects that have an energy form attached to them, often by their owners, which makes it difficult to get rid of them, or to do anything with the physical object because it would involve too much emotional pain to the owner.

People do this naturally and automatically; when this goes wrong due to stress and disturbances, it can lead to "collections" and also hoarding and fetish creation.

Here is an example of how working with the energy of an object can transform a difficult artefact into something that the owner has control of once more, and feels better about.

This was a lady who was moving house and had a huge collection of books which she could not take with her. She was distraught as she loved each and every one of them and this was "breaking her heart."

In a telephone session, an EMO practitioner helped the lady take into herself the energy from the first book, a particularly beloved first edition, EMO it in, through and out until the lady felt the EMO Energized End State and understood what her attachment to the book was about. She did another three books with the practitioner, then she did the rest of the books all together in an afternoon by herself and felt "that I've taken with me more than ever was written in all those books."

A gentleman who was hoarding old newspapers to the degree that his bungalow was filled with them floor to ceiling, leaving only narrow walkways between the front door and one other room now, felt the pain of putting a newspaper into the trash "as though my heart was being ripped out of my chest and I can't breathe." Ten minutes of EMO later, and he realised what the papers were all about (the hoarding had begun with the death of his father, and then gone completely out of control when his mother died whom he had cared for all his adult life).

Another thirty minutes later and he was not just ready and willing but even joyful to clear out all that paper and to find a new life for himself.

There are many problems relating to artefacts which simply can't be solved at all, and never mind humanely, if the energy system isn't taken into consideration. When we apply the right method to the right aspects of the human system, such as is the case with EMO and emotional problems, things become very simple and change and evolution can be had.

EMO puts you back in control of your earthly possessions and all your artefacts. This also applies to the acquisition of new artefacts. Often we find that if we work with the energy of an object at the point where we feel we want to buy and own it, the energy was all that was ever required in the first place. We got our energy boost and now we don't need to buy the object, saving us space, money, and all that effort dusting, carrying and managing the object in the future. When we have an experience where we EMO the energy of an object and come out of that wanting it even more than before, that's a good time to buy it and to take it home.

If you try that for a month, you'll be surprised how rare that is though; over 90% of the time, purchases are really about energy and not about material ownership.

EMO and Beliefs

When we first created EMO, we only wanted to change negative emotions and offer people an easy way to stop suffering from the pain of emotions as quickly as possible.

Then we found that when the energy system works better, cognitive changes - mind changes - occur naturally and as a side effect of the energy work that was done.

This is turn alerted us to the fact that an expression of a limiting belief, such as "I'll never get promoted, I don't have what it takes ..." is actually a verbal form of "Show me with your hands!" - the person is telling us where they have a snafu in their system, a blockage or an injury that causes them to feel that way, and the negative belief is the comment on that feeling.

Therefore, any limiting belief at all or any negative self belief is an expression of a disturbance in the energy system, and this being so, it is also "only an energy" and we can use EMO to make changes in negative beliefs.

Here is an example of changing a limiting belief.

P: "I'll never get promoted. I'm just not a team player, I'm not what they're looking for. I don't have what it takes."

Energist: "Where do you feel that in your body when you think about that? Show me with your hands."

P: Indicates just below the beginning of the neck, just above the collar bones, with a sideways movement of the hands, as though he was cutting his own throat.

Energist: "Tell me a bit more about the feeling."

P: "It feels - hard, stuck. Like it's the end, that's it, I can go no further."

238

Energist: "That sounds like an energy that wants to move upwards but it can go no further because there's some kind of block there ..."

P: "Yes, yes that's exactly what it feels like. And then I think, what's the point, this is as far as I will ever go."

Energist: "Ah but it's only an energy. Put your hands there where it stops, that's where the blockage is, take a deep breath. Very good. Now you focus on it from the inside and I'll help from the outside, and both of us soften that energy up, say soften and flow."

P: "Soften and flow." Coughs.

Energist: "That's really good. Keep breathing and use your hands to massage that erea, help unblock it."

P: Coughs. Coughs again.

Energist: "What's happening?"

P: "I can feel something tickling in my throat. (Coughs) There's something rising up my throat ..."

Energist: "Excellent! The energy is starting to move and that's making you cough. That probably means we need to soften it up more, it's still a bit stodgy. Keep breathing deeply and use your hands very gently to massage the era, keep thinking, soften and flow ..."

P: "Yes that's better, I can now feel it - my chest is getting warm. Is that normal?"

Energist: "When we start to improve the energy flow, we often feel it in different ways. Warm is usually good, it means there's life coming into it. How is it going in your throat?"

P: "It's definitely rising up now, I can feel it in my nose! (Rubs his nose) It tickles a bit but it doesn't hurt. Feels kinda funny."

Energist: "Excellent! It wants to go upward, that much we can know. Let it soften some more, let's find out the pathway. It needs to come out somewhere, there is an exit point somewhere."

P: "It's going up into my head, my forehead feels really strange, swirling, like fog."

Energist: "Nearly there, you're doing an excellent job. Yes, that's right, use your hands on your forehead, encourage the energy to find the path that leads out so it can leave your body."

P (Stroking up his forehead into his hair): "I think it needs to go out the top of my head, straight up."

Energist: "Keep breathing, soften and flow, let it flow out. How is that now?"

P: "Yes, I can feel it, I can feel it all the way from my chest like a column and its going out of the top of my head. Oh that is making me shiver! Oh wow that feels so strange!" (starts to smile and move).

Energist: "Very good! That's great! That's exactly right, you keep moving and encourage the flow, there can be quite a lot of energy that was trapped behind that erea that needs to come out ..."

P: "Yes! Yes I can really feel that - it feels ... amazing ..."

Energist: "Awesome job! Ok, now, take a deep breath - what about that not getting promoted? How do you feel about that now?"

P (Laughs out aloud): "That's ... that was just ... sad! Poor me! Why did I ever think that? Of course I can get promoted. I've got lots of ideas, lots more to give! I've held back all this time and I have no idea why - what was I thinking?"

Energist: "You felt like that because of the blockage in your throat. Now that it's gone, you don't think that any more. And how about not being a team player?"

P (Laughs): "I can play! In a team and out. Man, I feel so good! Is this going to last?"

Energist: "You can bring it back any time by making sure the energy runs up and your throat doesn't get blocked up again."

P (Makes the movements showing he is doing that from the chest up to the head and out): "That's awesome, that feels amazing ... Thank you so much!"

As in this example, you will often find that how the limiting beliefs are expressed in words and metaphors are reflected in the existing REAL injury or blockage in the energy system.

EMO is the fastest and most reliable changer of negative beliefs I know; it goes directly to the core of the problem, it is always healthy so by all means, make a list of your own limiting beliefs and treat them as soon as possible. With clients and other people, using the direct body feedback to change the negative beliefs is a wonderful short cut and you don't ever need to know where those came from; simply enjoy the fact that once they're gone, you feel better, brighter and you act and think far more rationally.

EMO and Body Image

The basic body image or body concept a person has is probably the most powerful factor in whether they consider themselves to be able to achieve love and success across the board in this life time.

The body image often reflects existing conditions in the energy system; people can have truly severe injuries in the energy body and the related body parts become a focus of dissatisfaction, self hatred, and negative feelings and emotions.

Now this is structurally correct; a person who experiences strong negative feelings when they consider their nose, for example, is supposed to be guided to an injury in that area that needs healing and treatment. These signals are completely misunderstood and people turn to plastic surgery, when a little energy healing would do the trick so easily and let the nose by a perfectly good nose at every level again.

In energy work, a host of behaviours and emotions relating to body image and self concept make perfect sense when without taking energy into consideration, they seem bizarre or insane. For example in anorexia, where a person "feels fat" even though they are literally dying of starvation, until and unless something is done about the conditions of the energy body, which may well be fat and swollen due to blockages and pent up energy, little can be achieved.

This is such an important and essential topic that we have devoted an entire additional training programme that uses advanced EMO to this topic. It is called BeautyT and I would consider this essential information for anyone who deals with people who have emotional disturbances relating to their body image.

In one way or the other, every person in the Western world at least does have emotional disturbances relating to their own bodies; and much evolution towards becoming a happier person, a more confident person can be achieved by doing EMO with negative emotions relating to our own bodies.

242

In general, keep it simple when working with your own or another person's body image. Simply ask if there is something about themselves that they don't like, just as a plastic surgeon would. If there's a long, long list, take one thing at a time, starting with the first thing they said, such as, "My nose is too big." Then run the normal EMO protocol on where they feel that in their body and move the energy to an EMO Energized End State, at which point the nose will have become not just of normal size, but actually, a beloved and fully integrated functional part of the human totality.

- ***For further information about BeautyT - EMO for the Body Image please see: BeautyT Manual & Self Help CD, and BeautyT Workshop Recordings, both available from*** DragonRising.com

EMO and Bereavement

Bereavement pain, deep grief or sorrow, is the strongest and most painful of all human emotions, and like all emotions, bereavement pain makes no sense at all - unless you bring the energy system, the true Factor X of the human condition, into the equation.

Bereavement pain isn't in the head - it is an actual felt pain in the body that comes in waves and can be totally debilitating.

Pop psychology doesn't help by labelling the various forms this pain takes from day to day as "anger" or "guilt" or even "survivor guilt", and there is also that very unhelpful and even downright cruel underlying suggestion, always lurking in the background, that the person who suffers from bereavement pain doesn't "want" to get better, "wants" to suffer or is trying to "hold on" to their suffering - making it all their fault on top of everything else.

When we consider that people really do have an energy body, and that this energy body sends messages, signals of pain (and of pleasure) to let people know how it's doing, then bereavement pain makes perfect sense.

People make energetic connections by nature - this is how we "connect," this is how we interact, how we love and this is also how we learn.

The strongest energetic connection is that between a mother and her child, because their systems were one at one point, and only gradually do these connections grow apart; but some of them never do and they will remain over time and space, no matter what.

The second strongest form of connection is that between twins, life partners or other people who have lived together for a very long time. Spending a lot of time in each other's company strengthens and deepens these energetic connections; and in very close relationships and families, the energy systems merge into one - they grow together and form couple bubbles and group bubbles.

So you can imagine that if you tear someone out of this exquisite, fragile web of energetic connections, it is going to cause tremendous pain. This is the bereavement pain we can feel in our bodies, and which can cause physical illness, if these injuries in the energy system, where the other was "torn away", aren't healed, and healed quickly. For a person in bereavement, it really is as though parts of their insides have been torn away, and their life force is bleeding out of these injuries.

When we ask a person directly, "Where is the worst pain? Where do you really feel it in your body? Show me with your hands!" the person who suffers from bereavement pain responds by, first of all, being relieved that someone finally is dealing with the real crux of the matter - the pain from the injuries they are carrying.

It can happen that people can be in therapy for years, decades even, and that question was never asked, the actual pain of bereavement never directly addressed.

Now, the person is holding their hands to their chest.

"This is where the pain is," they say, "It is so bad I can hardly breathe ..."

We can look at the place they are showing us with their hands, and now we know where the worst injury is located. Often, there are more ereas of injury; but just like with a multiple gunshot victim brought into the ER, it is the most dangerous wound, the most painful one, we treat first; and when that is done and the patient is stabilised, we treat the others, one by one, in order of severity.

The energy body is injured, we must heal the energy body, and as soon as possible, so that our patient doesn't develop serious ill health (you could think of this like an infection that will infest an untreated wound, and ultimately lead to the patient's demise!).

How do we heal the energy body? The good news is that as everyone has an energy body, we also all have "healing hands" or energy hands which can touch the energy body.

245

Even better, we also have an "energy mind" (previously known as the unconscious or subconscious mind) which can which knows what to do.

All "we" have to do - our conscious selves - is to hold the intention of healing that wound that is causing the bereavement pain.

We say to the person, "I am going to place my attention on that place from the outside, and you help from the inside, and let's find out if we can't make this any better."

We can hold our hands to that place, but we must remember that it isn't our physical hands that are doing the healing, it is the hands of energy that everyone has which are doing the work.

We can ask the person to breathe deeply and to let energy flow into that injured erea so it can start to rebuild itself, so it can start to heal.

The wonderful thing about this way of working is that no one ever says, "I don't want to do that, I want to keep suffering ..."

There is no "psychology" involved - we are simply healing an injury, and nothing more.

And the results speak for themselves.

More, self healing now becomes not only possible, but is the right thing to do.

We know exactly where it hurts the most. We can put our own healing hands there, stroking, soothing, asking for the energy flow to be restored, for healing to take place.

It is the most natural thing in the world to be doing, and it is the right thing - and the proof is that it works.

To understand that bereavement pain is real, that you are not crazy, that this isn't all in your mind or you're making it up somehow, but that you really have an injury that needs healing is a huge relief for many people who suffer from bereavement pain already.

The real relief comes, however, once the healing starts.

Once the pain starts to soften, and the previous waves of bereavement pain start to ebb away.

The most telling aspect of it all however and at the end of the day is the fact that as we are really healing that which is really injured, there is NO shame, NO guilt, NO anger - only an ever gathering sense of love, and appreciation for those who were lost in body but are still very much with us in spirit, that grows in strength at the same time as the pain fades until there is only love left, and love is all there is.

That is our final proof that we did the right thing, and we really did find the answer to bereavement pain.

- If you suffer from intense bereavement pain, a session with an EMO Master Practitioner is advised. EMO doesn't hurt, and it has helped many more than words can say.

- Be kind to yourself. Remember that you're not crazy, you're injured, and you need to heal.

- Use your own healing hands. Focus on the will to heal, breathe deeply.

- If you have a spiritual light you can turn towards, ask their help to heal this injury as well.

- Accept assistance from others to heal this injury. Even little children have powerful healing hands, often much more so than adults.

- You know when you are healed when there is no more pain left, no more sadness, no regrets and all that remains is love.

This final step is absent from current psychological bereavement lore; we call the healed stage of bereavement "The immortal beloved" who is always with you.

EMO and Business

EMO has many significant applications in the business world which also runs on, by and over human emotions. When there are emotional disturbances, the Even Flow of the business will suffer as the human components of the system that is the business overall start to malfunction.

This sounds less than holistic; but when you explain it like that, even hard nosed business people (what kind of energy form might be stuck there, and has become so hard it was enshrined thus in a metaphor for all business people?) will understand that adding extra energy and enthusiasm in their workforce on the one hand, and taking out emotional reversals which cause stress, absenteeism and inadequate performance as well as interpersonal strife will absolutely add precious dollars to their bottom line.

There are many practical advantages to using EMO in business.

The first is that EMO is logical, can be felt, is immediately effective to change emotions with very little practice, it is structural and therefore accessible to people who would strongly reject more esoteric ideas such as yoga or meditation.

"Where do you feel that pressure rising in your body when you are under stress?" is a simple question that, once answered and this pressure has been released using the incredibly simple and straightforward EMO method, can save a large company millions of dollars by preventing their workforce getting sick with stress.

There is more to that, however. Stressed people make very bad decisions; and the more stressed they are, the more mistakes pile up and the more disastrous the decisions become. It is of the essence for a really well run business to perform at its best that the main decision makers know how to free themselves from stress and how to find additional energy as and when required. This holds true for a one man business just the same as it does for a huge multi-national business; keeping the best decision makers stress free and working logically is clearly of the essence.

248

Similarly, for creatives at any level of any business to do their best work, they too need to be stress free and flowing smoothly. Creative endeavours absolutely rely on an incoming data stream from the energy mind - visions and ideas, flashes of insight - which is severely disturbed by stress. When EMO is applied with a creative project in mind, the additional energy and information brings about breakthrough insights due to the dual action of firstly de-stressing the creative, and secondly enhancing energy and information flow throughout their systems.

For highly competitive and secretive businesses, the "secret therapy" features of EMO, meaning that the reasons or causes of the existing problem do not have to be named and nothing has to be discussed is a bonus that is not found in other forms of helping especially top executives and the keepers of the secrets of a company with releasing their stress.

EMO can help transform the effectiveness of sales people by firstly, improving their relationship with the products and services they are supposed to sell; secondly, by improving their relationships with potential customers; and thirdly, by working on their beliefs regarding just how good a salesperson they are and how much they can achieve. Helping sales people release emotional injuries from past bad experiences, such as incidences of rejection or aggression, also improves sales performances and reduces stress in the sales force.

There are many, many more applications of EMO to business; from removing shields to customers to allow for better communication in the sales force to helping improve the performance in workers and managers, there are practical, powerful applications of EMO that can help a business succeed and develop to a whole new level of effectiveness.

On a more structural level, considering a business as an energy system in its own right and track the energy flow of operations (goods, products, staff, money) in, through and out can highlight problem ereas in the business.

Solutions can be found and implemented to make the entire business entity work much, much better.

A modern energist is in fact a systems engineer. This skill set can be applied across the logical levels of a business, to find the business entity's own even flow overall, in a department, in a board room, in a sub group.

The applications for EMO and the additional information that gives a far more complete and reality based assessment of what is really going on (with the building, with the marketing department, with Mr Smith, with the call centre operators, with the products, with the customer service, etc. etc. etc ...) is priceless.

EMO and Child Abuse Survivors

A psychologist wrote to me and asked if EMO was "suitable to use with child abuse survivors". This is what I told them.

I'm also a child abuse survivor and I can attest to the fact that EMO is the gentlest and at the same time, the most powerful form of dealing with the very real "feelings" one is often overcome by, in real time and in the real world.

Indeed, the fact that you don't have to remember anything, re-live anything, actively forgive anything, and for once you can just go with what your body and your feelings are telling you, and it doesn't matter "if it's real or just imagined," has been a complete godsend to me personally and proven its value and practical helpfulness in many different contexts.

Now child abuse is a wide and varied thing; it's difficult because the memories as to the exact sequences of events, police memories if you will, are often unclear, skewed, seen through a child's eyes and sometimes just not there, at least not at the top conscious level.

You get dreams and nightmares too, weird flashbacks and all sorts of thoughts over the years and in the end you don't known at all what's what - only that you have all these symptoms and you know something went on that was deeply disturbing.

It is true that one of the reasons I was looking for something that did not rely on conscious awareness and the ability to come up with exact and precise opening statements is because of my personal experiences.

To be able to "cut out all the talk" - and with that, all the justifications, the reasons, the possible flaws in the memories and the arguments, the conflicts and the fear of what else might be there - was a positive GODSEND to me. After all these years, I was tired of telling and talking. I was tired of even thinking about how and if and what. I was tired of remembering and trying to remember. It

251

got me nowhere and often, I used to think, "My God that was nearly half a century ago - will it ever be over?!"

EMO works with energy and this explains why time wasn't healing this - the energy system is timeless in essence, all things are here and now, and until and unless something is done to change the conditions of the energy system, things will remain just as they were forever.

*At the same time, there is the other side of the coin. All "that" isn't here any longer. It is all gone, long gone and the only place in which these injuries still exist are indeed, in the energy system. That is a wonderfully soothing thought, and when waves of painful emotions hit you, to be able to think, "This is **ONLY AN ENERGY** now, and there is something I can do about that!" has been a revelation to me and so many others.*

To be able to validate my "weird" emotional responses to "perfectly normal" situations was also immensely helpful. In EMO we take the point of view that we were only dealing with energy now and disturbances in the energy system; this allowed me to accept the emotions, feelings and sensations for what they really were: cries for help, the sign posts to direct me straight towards what needed healing and restoring.

For the first time, rather than having to switch off my body sensations, I could finally listen to them, acknowledge them and use them for arrow straight guided self healing.

Starting to actively pay attention to my physical feelings which are what emotions really are got me "back into the body" for the first time in 45 years. The body was no longer the enemy; instead, it had become a system crying out for help, and finally, these cries for help could be heard, and then answered with action. This action starts with a healing intention and all else flows from there.

Further, the act of listening and paying attention to the actual body sensations that we call feelings and emotions is the perfect guideline to your own custom made healing therapy. As each

252

sensation emerges and is dealt with, the healing process unfolds under its own steam, in its own ecology, in the right order and sequence and without fear or any kind of major abreaction, major operations, re-traumatizing flashbacks and entirely in harmony with every individual person and their particular needs.

EMO is amazing in its presuppositions and in how it works.

There's nothing quite like it, and the totally non-judgemental nature of all its workings, which for some people seems strange and even sometimes too logical and systemic, is exactly what the doctor ordered for child abuse survivors, and especially child sex abuse survivors.

Any healing modality that is going to work with child sex abuse survivors has to be absolutely systemic and non-judgemental or else the aspects who hold all that shame and guilt and grief and anger simply cannot benefit from any healing - they are structurally excluded "because they don't deserve to be healed."

And of course, I don't even want to begin to start talking about the aspects who may have identified with the abuser/s, loved them, connected to them or patterned themselves on them in some way - those never get a look in in the standard approaches of psychotherapy and many other doctrines of psychology and spiritual healing.

In EMO, we don't have "good" or "bad" energies. All is only energy. That's just like you can't stand in the rain, watch the raindrops go by and point a finger and say, "Look there goes another bad one!"

This is the concept of "innocent energy" - rain will fall on an abuser and their victims, on the grass and the mountains just the same, it makes no judgement either way. For abuse survivors, this concept can be life saving, for every abuse survivor is both the abuser and the victim in one person.

In EMO, we don't have to struggle for forgiveness or self forgiveness. The whole concept dissolves the moment the pain is gone - once that happens, forgiveness comes into being. It is important to understand that it is structurally impossible to forgive yourself or any other whilst you are still in acute pain. When the pain has ceased, forgiveness arises naturally - and not one moment earlier.

We can call our emotions what we like - shame, guilt, anger, fear, sadness, depression; but in the end, these are all just pain deriving from injuries in the energy system.

Pain we feel in our bodies, pain which shows us where we need to direct our healing intention and our healing energy.

It is true that when I first began to experiment with EMO, I had no idea that it would do so much more than just really heal the worst forms of emotional pain. To even find some minor relief for this everlasting chronic suffering that child abuse survivors have learned to live with somehow would have been akin to a miracle to me.

But EMO goes much, much further than that.

There is another side, something beyond "just not feeling the pain any more".

Once we begin to listen to the body again and end the withdrawal from the physical, to our amazement we find that the body can send us other kinds of feedback about the energy system - the good feelings. When the energy system is working once more as it should, as it was designed to work by the Creative Order, and we have learned to listen again, we become the recipients of wonderful gifts. Feelings of joy, of energies rushing through your body, making you tingle, making you feel alive and powerful, opening your eyes to the beauty of the world and your place within it - it is extraordinary to come home to that at last.

That is the greatest gift of EMO for me - to end my long exile and allow me to come home to Creation itself.

All the re-unification processes of EMO, all the weight on the systemic nature and structure of injuries in the energy system and how they relate firstly to emotion, and from there manifest in thought and behaviour that are at the core of EMO were first of all road tested right there - in the abuse survivor scenarios, in the high end trenches of psychological and energetic disturbance that have lasted a lifetime.

Further still, the "client/practitioner dance" at the heart of the co-joint healing endeavour between two equals, where the "healer" is literally forbidden to tell anyone what is wrong with them, how they should be feeling, and where the healers are only allowed to focus on "putting to right what once went wrong," only follow along with the person's own special unfoldments and even then, only when and if the person in question is ready and willing, all that is patterned directly on the needs of child abuse survivors.

Of course, these "fail safes" build right into the very structure of EMO are of benefit to anyone at all, and it doesn't matter why they are in pain or where they got their disturbances from, we don't judge, we only heal.

EMO is not an instant miracle cure for child abuse survivors; but I can personally attest to the fact that every aspect of its theory, workings, structure and how EMO is conducted is designed to help child abuse survivors finally find relief for their emotions and injuries, and to put them on the road to have all the pleasures of life, all the wonderful experiences of the body, back in their reach when it seemed so impossible before.

EMO and Children

The way children do EMO is just extraordinary; you have to try it to find out for yourself how easy and simple it is for them to "let that swirling in my belly run down and into my legs and out."

Indeed, the fact that children can do EMO so easily and readily was one of my own personal convincers that we were on the right track with the idea that emotions really are only an energy movement, and that we humans can change the course of these movements by the application of conscious intention.

Nowadays, when I find an adult all reversed and locked down who tells me that EMO is too much too ask, too difficult, requires too much of a leap of faith, is too "out there" I sigh and think of the children. I soften and flow, look at the adult opposite and I might ask, "Have you ever felt a powerful emotion in your body, perhaps when you were younger than you are today ...?"

When we stop judging children for emotionally driven behaviours, and instead take the EMO point of view that "it is only an energy," wonderful things happen.

As caretakers of children and youngsters we stop taking what they do and say so personally. We become aware how stress builds up in children, and how different children are already showing such different ways in which to demonstrate where their reversals and blockages are located. We become more knowledgeable and far more compassionate, towards the children in the here and now, but also importantly, towards the children that each one of us were, once upon a time.

When we become energy aware, we start to understand the principles of attention seeking behaviour; and we become aware that attention is something children need to grow strong, happy energy bodies, just as they need good food to grow strong, happy physical bodies.

When we understand that, we stop giving the children in our environment a poverty diet that leaves them angry, hungry, whining and unfulfilled day in, day out.

We learn that focused, positive attention isn't a long haul of hours and hours at a time; but that there are moments where one flash of attention, given exactly when asked for, transforms everything - transforms the energy system of the child, makes the child happy, makes you happy.

Energy is free and when it is freely given as and when it is asked for, relationships blossom.

If people only understood the simple rule from the Harmony Program which states that attention given when it is asked for will in and of itself, completely collapse unfolding attention seeking behaviour disturbances at their very root so they never happen or escalate at all, the world of child care and parenting would be a different place, and a better place for any child to grow up in.

There is a fictional greeting from the movie Avatar whereby people say to each other, "I see you," by the way of a greeting. It means not just that they see them with their physical eyes, but take the whole of that other person into their awareness - a real EMO movement of dropping shields that are getting in the way, and taking the energy of that person in, through and out. I invite you to try this simple method of focusing on people in general, not just children, before you interact with them, and whenever you become aware someone is seeking your attention.

Stop for a moment, turn to look at them and think to yourself, "I see you," without saying anything at all. Then notice what happens next. Often, this one real true contact is all that was needed and the person will walk away, happy and satisfied, with their energy system having been re-balanced by the contact with you.

This works for all and everything that seeks your attention in its own special way; but with children, it is particularly crucial that this should be learned and implemented wherever possible.

Children should also be encouraged to become energy aware from their end, so that they can notice when their care takers are going out of Even Flow and into reversals. Knowing that mummy said something mean because she had some energy thing going wrong in her chest, rather than because the child is evil, makes a lot of difference to the self concept of a child, especially over the long haul.

It opens the door for children to become the healers of their parents too, and I am very serious about that. Children too have hands of energy, and their energy systems are wonderfully pure in comparison to that of adults; it is a completely different type of energy they produce from where they are. So if you have a headache, and feel a pressure in the back of your head, and there's a handy child in your environment that can be safely invited to put their little hands on the erea where it hurts the most, prepare to be astonished what that feels like.

Teenagers too are well renown for having such huge energy emissions that they create poltergeist effects in their environment; so by all means, if you have one of those, let their healing hands do the world of good to you by simply asking them for a touch in the right place and at the right time.

People are designed and programmed by nature to help each other. We have 98% DNA shared with chimpanzees who groom each other all the time, touch each other all the time, will come to the assistance of one amongst them who seems sad or in pain.

Giving children the power back to change your states, to change your mind, and allow them the joy of having helped and made a difference in the world is a gift beyond measure.

I would like to add that to look at a child's creative template and use that as a guiding device, rather than some set ideas or prejudices of what any child or youngster, or any person could or should be or become, makes an enormous difference for parents and grandparents, and for the child, who is being seen by someone at last.

For parents in a moment of crisis, when they are very worried about the child, to tune into the creative template is an instant stabiliser and can help more than I have words to say; I know this from personal experience.

There is so much else I could tell you about in regards to children, our own, those of other people and the children we once were and who still live in our memories and in our energy matrix; but if you follow the simple rules of EMO and become more energy aware, learn in your own time and from your own experiences, you can't go far wrong.

The rewards are immeasurable, and ripply ever further over time.

EMO and Confidence

In the past, people who have "tried to improve their confidence" have worried endlessly about whether just feeling confident without having the real skills to back it up with the required actions wouldn't be a very bad thing, and so it might be better to not artificially feel confident when one shouldn't feel confident ...

These kinds of contortions simply disappear when we apply EMO and move a person towards their own Even Flow.

Having an energized and well working energy body that makes one feel strong, powerful and capable doesn't lead into any kind of delusion - in the contrary, it puts one in exactly the right position to judge cleanly and logically if one has the skills to do a thing, or not, and make a very informed decision.

So you can be fully confident that any improvement in confidence you obtain through the practice of EMO is good confidence!

Confidence is situation specific and that's how we apply the EMO treatment. Most people are pretty confident already that they can make themselves a cup of tea or get a beer from the fridge; a collapse in the energy system that is experienced as "a loss of confidence" occurs in direct response to some kind of trigger or some kind of particular situation.

So we can ask, "When do you feel you're not confident? When does that happen?" and a person may say, "It happens when I have to speak to the bank manager about a loan."

Now we have a specific situation, and we can find a specific location by asking, "And where do you feel that in your body when you think about going to see the bank manager?" This is actually a real life example; this really happened. After the EMO Energized End State had been achieved, the person was able to reflect that they didn't know enough about their own personal finances in detail, and that to be prepared properly for the meeting, they should at least consult last month's bank statements, which they had avoided because it hurt to look at them! This made both the practitioner and the person laugh at some length, then a bank statement was produced which looked "very clear, very sharply defined, it's just numbers, I really need to take more control of that ..."

Every EMO session for "confidence" is different for every person; if you stay specific rather than too global and nebulous and focus on those moments when you can feel your confidence or rather, the strength of your energy body that powers you through life, starts to fail, great progress can be made and real confidence, reality based confidence, emerges "as if by magic."

EMO and Crystals

People who have no energy awareness often denigrate the New Age fascination with crystals, declaring them to be nothing more than rocks and all the rest is "only in the mind."

When you do start to have energy awareness, you'll notice that crystals and their effects is not just in the mind, but in the body too; crystals are in fact the perfect training objects for people who have trouble feeling energy in their bodies.

I first experienced this many, many years ago when I was helping out selling some crystals in a German street market. People became attracted to the shining, glittering crystals and I would ask them to hold one and feel the energy moving up into their arms. Entirely energy unaware good German burgers would jump in surprise, eyes wide open, astonished and shout out, "I really felt that!"

I took that original experience to an EMO Conference and gave the participants a variety of crystals to play with in the sunshine; and when you add a little EMO to the experience mix, of course, many people fell in love with crystals for the first time, and others discovered whole new realms of crystal-induced experiences they had not expected even existed.

Crystals, as there are so many different kinds, and as each one in itself is entirely unique and has therefore, a unique energy all of its own, are a great practice partner for energy awareness and to help develop fine tune our precious 6th sense.

The simple EMO question of "Where do you feel this particular crystal in your body?" produces all sorts of different sensations for different crystals; delightful tingles here and there, sometimes powerful responses, sometimes pain. The latter is helpful because when a crystal causes pain, that denotes a blockage and we can use that very crystal to provide the energy to help soften and flow that erea and reach a wonderful EMO Energized End State.

Crystals are of course, entirely unconditional; and it is easy to conceptualise that and accept that. As such, they can slide through shields to people, to plants, to animals; crystals can go places in the energy system where no other energy can reach.

Going to a crystal shop, or to your own crystal collection and asking, "Which one is the best to help me, right now, for this one problem?" and then paying attention to your 6th sense, your body sensations that will guide you in the right direction without fail, is an excellent way of improving both energy flow as well as energy awareness.

Combinations of crystals produce what I call "the crystal song" - a cocktail of energies that can blow you away with the wonderful experiences this produces.

If you work with EMO on a professional basis, having a few crystals around that your energy body has expressed to you are fit for the purpose, and having a client hold those and track how this energy moves into, through and out of their bodies, and how you can really feel that, can provide a breakthrough experience for people who would otherwise have walked away, thinking they "can't do energy" - just like the German burgers who were so surprised and then delighted that they could really feel something, a little miracle gift from the true wonderworlds of energy that has the power to change lives in the long run.

EMO and Depression

If you think about it, depression with all its symptoms is the exact opposite of the EMO Energized End State in mind, body and spirit, and this gives us immediate guidance on how to approach healing what is called depression through pure energy work.

First of all, any depression comes from somewhere. There is a reason, there is a time when it started, there is an event that caused a major injury in the energy system which remained untreated at the time, still remains untreated and is the direct cause for all the mind, body, spirit symptoms of depression that result from that.

This is a significant type of injury that is big enough and painful enough so it is virtually impossible to not find it, and for a person to not know where that is located in their bodies.

Energy healing for this injury is the first and most urgent directive in the treatment of depression. This can be augmented and supported by good daily energy practice and especially by Heart Healing on a regular basis; often (but not always) there is heartbreak involved in the formation of depression.

I would also like to add the comment that depressed people and those in their environment often wrongly assume that they need more energy coming in.

Depression occurs because there is no or too little movement in the energy system; this is caused by the original injury which preceded the onset of the depression. Adding in more energy which is likewise getting stuck behind that injury only serves to increase the pressure and makes the depression symptoms even worse; this is why depressed people have to withdraw from human interaction and other naturally energizing behaviours such as exercise and enjoying the powerful energies of sunshine, sex or art.

Until and unless the injury is treated, and energy flow in the energy body has been restored, adding additional energy is counter

264

productive. Once the injury has been treated, daily energy practice and keeping the flow in that particular erea supported in times of stress and trouble opens the door for other energizing experiences once more.

There is one more piece of good news for the treatment of depression. In talking therapy, you don't get very far if a person is taking psychopharmaca, medication often prescribed against depression, because of the confusing effects this has on the mind.

EMO doesn't require people to be on the ball with words and memories; the injury in the person's energy system is entirely real and it doesn't matter if that person is tranquillized or not in order to repair this. The practitioner will have to do more work and pull their weight a little more with additional effort on their side and also, to keep an easily de-focused client on track who might need more time, more positive feedback and more encouragement all along the way, but an injured energy system is an injured energy system and it will respond to energy healing as normal.

I liken this to being able to operate on a gun shot wound regardless of whether the person is conscious or not; we are not dealing with imagination in EMO, but with real energy work, so this is especially good news for people who have been told that because they had to resort to taking medication in their desperation, they can't find healing until they've given up taking them.

Also, working with the relationship between a person and their medication can significantly reduce side effects and many psychosomatic symptoms and makes a gradual removal in conjunction with the prescribing physician's advice much easier as well.

EMO, Classic EFT and Energy EFT

The original Classic EFT or Emotional Freedom Techniques was orginally developed by Gary Craig from the US and is a popular modern energy psychology method that works by making an opening statement for the problem, thereby connecting with the problem, and tapping on a selection of important points which relate to major body meridians.

There are only a few of these tapping points, which include the top of the head, the third eye point, the beginning of the eyebrow at the bridge of the nose, the bone on the outside of the corner of the eye, under the eye, under the nose, under the mouth, in the corner of the collarbones, on the side of the body in line with a man's nipples, and the hand points which are on the inside when you look at your hands, on the side of each finger in line with where the nail starts, plus a point on the side of the hand called the Karate Chop point which is said to help with global energy reversals.

EMO is fundamental to the development of modern Energy EFT, so here is an essay from 2011 that traces the lineage of the different techniques and approaches utilized in Energy EFT back to EMO Energy In Motion.

EMO's Gifts To EFT

Silvia Hartmann wrote in November 2011: I've spent the last 6 months doing nothing but writing the new GoE Energy EFT Master Practitioner training courses for live trainings and distance learning certification.

"Why?" we may ask, seeing that in EMO we already have highly advanced modern energy work at our fingertips. This is a good question.

As the chairman of The GoE, I have to look after all modern energy modalities and techniques, not just my own; that's one part of it.

Another part is that there are a lot of people out there who want quality, professional EFT trainings on the one hand, and the GoE trainers wanted a state-of-the-art, brand new EFT training for all the people who are asking them for EFT courses on the other. This is a good thing in every way. I too really enjoyed EFT when it first came out and certainly did my bit to publicise it in the UK and through the Internet worldwide.

I made the leap to EMO after five years of intensive Classic EFT work. EMO is not so much a healing modality (although it can do that too, and very well indeed at that) but primarily, EMO is a tool for finding out more about the principles of real energy work across the board.

As a result, we did find out a great many things that simply were not known or as clearly described as they are now in the practice of EMO. Now, when it came to the new EFT training, I could have withheld these and left them for EMO exclusively; but that's not in the spirit of the thing. My purpose is to improve energy awareness; that's my major mission. To have people understand that energy work is either entirely real.

Energy exists or at the very least, we can use the word "energy" as a place holder or a metaphor that works so well for human beings, we

267

simply can't be doing without it in order to understand reality *at all*.

So I did say that I would agree to spend that much precious time of my life on writing a new EFT course - but only if it was going to be an EFT course which would incorporate what we had learned about real energy work through the practice of EMO.

As you can imagine, that radical approach produced a few gasps and still does; but if I weigh up stepping on a few toes against taking EFT to the next level of effectiveness, of precision, of predictability and of *sheer enjoyment,* then so be it.

Here is a short round up of the "gifts of EMO" the new Energy EFT Master Practitioner course has received.

Putting Energy Into EFT

First and foremostly amongst all, it is the declaration that Energy EFT is not psychology, it is not psychotherapy, it is not hypnosis, it is not kinesiology, but instead, it is ENERGY WORK.

Even though we are tapping our faces, bodies and hands with our material fingers, it is the energy fingers touching the energy body that creates the changes in EFT, pure and simple.

This is a complete game changer when it comes to how we approach every aspect of the treatment flow of the EFT session, from the practitioner preparing themselves to receiving the client, every step of the way, to the final farewell at the end and beyond into the ongoing client/practitioner relationship.

When we think in terms of energy work, and energy flow through the session itself, then through the practitioner and the client and how all of that works together, we naturally come to different ways of thinking about the EFT session.

We begin to notice where there are ZZZTs in the treatment flow itself; we can pinpoint blockages, reversals and disturbances in the treatment flow and take them out to produce a far smoother and more elegant (and in the end, more effective) EFT treatment experience.

That was the starting point to forward-engineering EFT into its new future as a proper energy modality, designed to create changes in the energy body.

The first thing that underwent consideration from this standpoint was the actual EFT protocol. The new energy based EFT protocol, called the Heart & Soul Protocol, is designed for maximum energy flow and ease of use, whilst retaining the essential tapping procedure that makes EFT what it is.

Heart Healing

The new EFT protocol includes a major gift from EMO: the Heart Healing posture. It provides centring at the start of the EFT round, and just as importantly, at the end, to give a space for the person to find their bearing after changes in the energy system took place. The Heart Healing posture also has some other interesting features.

As a "global reversal" cure, it is second to none; but it also draws out the healing hands, sets up a natural energy flow so that even people who have no idea and have never thought about their healing hands will be using their healing hands when they start to tap. This obviously improves the results of any single round of EFT considerably; and in the hands or fingertips of an experienced practitioner who knows what they are doing, improves results dramatically.

Having the Heart Healing posture to centre, stabilise and focus the person/client also allows us to drop the very confusing "Even though ... I deeply and profoundly love and accept myself," which was originally put in place to avoid abreactions as people start to tune in on their problems. It also caused a lot of conflict with many clients, and in neuro-linguistic terms really confuses the tuning in procedure, as we are no longer sure if we're focusing on "my fear of spiders" or "whether I profoundly love and accept myself."

The Heart Healing posture is also an excellent "mini energy moment" in its own right and EFTers who have learned to use it in conjunction with the tapping points as a part of the EFT round can use it to de-stress when they can't tap a full round.

I'd like to add that the feedback from people testing this out on themselves and EFT clients has been unanimously highly positive; beginners and experienced EFTers alike really appreciate the additional stabilisation framing the EFT round with the Heart Healing posture has brought.

The next important gift from EMO to EFT is:

270

The SUE Scale & The Healing Event

The SUE scale shows in a nutshell the difference between "old EFT" which was used with the then existing SUD scale (Subjective Units of Discomfort) and the new energy based EFT.

In the old paradigm, Zero was "as good as it gets" - pain cessation, not to be in pain anymore. This is fine when used for medical treatments; but in energy work, Zero is not as good as it gets. In fact, Zero is quite literally, nothing. In order to work with the energy system correctly, we need to improve energy flow into the POSITIVE range - this is the realm of positive emotions, high logic, full functioning, and full expression of a person's resources across the board.

The old SUD scale measures discomfort from -10 to 0 and there it stops. The new SUE Scale, which stands for Subject Units Of Experience, has an additional wing and so it spans from -10, maximum negative experience, to 0, feeling nothing, and then towards +10, which is a profoundly charged state of joy, love and happiness.

271

We have learned through EMO that when energy flow is increased to the point where it flows fast and powerfully, an "energized end state" comes into being - and the problem is solved, cured, it will never come back.

This "healing event" is achievable in EFT also, simply by evolving the energy flow from the original negative starting point further and further, one round of EFT at a time, until the healing event is reached at +10.

The healing event, what it is and how it works is a gift to EFT in so many ways. Firstly, its existence alone will now inspire EFTers to keep tapping and not stop too soon, just having shaved a few points of the pain is not enough any longer!

Secondly, we have now an explanation of the so called "One minute wonder" or "EFT miracle" occurrences. A healing event was reached quickly and that's what happened.

Thirdly, we can now say to EFTers that they don't have to feel out of control as far as these healing events are concerned any longer. Simply keep tapping the rounds and keep improving the energy flow. If you're lucky, you can get a surprise healing event along the way. If you are not, but you keep evolving the problem and improving the energy flow, eventually the healing event MUST happen - it can't not. And the healing event will happen when you have increased energy flow enough so it is in the high positives on the SUE scale.

This gives EFTers for the first time a clear, easy, doable and predictable path to the healing event; and of course, the slogan:

You don't have to solve it, only evolve it.

The Client/Practitioner Dance Becomes The EFTeam

The next gift from EMO to EFT is our learnings about the client/practitioner dance. We have learned that in energy work, you can't hide behind shields and "detach" yourself from the client to have it work as well as it should.

Indeed, the more engaged the practitioner and client can become, the more powerful the energy work becomes; and it also becomes a fantastic experience not just for the client, but also for the practitioner.

This is a super win/win/win/win situation as practitioners really do want to relate to their clients; as clients really do want to feel loved and supported, especially when they are scared and troubled; as clients begin to feel relief and relax, and the practitioner experiences this first hand, directly, in their own body and then also experiences together with the client the pure joy of the eventual resolution, and the wonderful energy sensations of the healing event shared by both equally.

The non-hierarchical, "team" based approach of EMO has become the EFTeam, and once again, the feedback from EFT practitioners old and young completely reflects the love EMO practitioners have had of this way of working with people and energy for the last ten years.

In energy work, getting into deep rapport or as we energists call it, to bubble with the client and working together to solve the problem as equals is simply the right thing to do; the modality demands it, and it is really inspiring for both clients and practitioners as well.

EMO also gave the gift of pre-testing what would happen if clients and practitioners form a powerful bubble as they connect up their energy fields and become more than the sum of their parts.

Over 10 years of practice, there was no problem with transference or countertransference *at all.* It simply - worked.

The 6th Sense, Mindful EFT & The EFT Body Protocol

Anyone who knows EMO will of course recognise where all these important additions to the practice of EFT as modern energy work are coming from.

Basic EMO practically unlocks our 6th sense - the sensing of movements in the energy body that have no physical origin.

For many EFTers, the Mindful EFT Protocol is the first time they have become consciously aware of energy sensations as they tap the points silently and scan their body to notice how tapping on one point produces all sorts of different body sensations compared to tapping on another. This is such an important breakthrough; for a person to experience the reality of energy *in their own body* is the starting point to a completely different approach to mind/body/spirit health and understanding.

For this reason, we now use this in the first teaching of Energy EFT in the foundation course. People who start out with this experience develop a profoundly different relationship with Energy EFT but also progress much faster in their studies.

The EFT Body Protocol, which is straight basic EMO with tapping the points, is also extremely important in this context.

It gives EFTers an excellent alternative to the complications of spoken set ups and reminder phrases which is so useful in the treatment of psychosomatic pain, pain in general, illness, recovery, and all those emotions that can't be named or explained in words at all. It also once again focuses the EFTers on the physical sensations of energy movements and thus helps them learn more about their 6th sense, which is a life skill.

Through the Body Protocol, some features of EMO such as "Secret Therapy" become available too and the Energy EFT practitioners conscious awareness of body movements, body postures, hand gestures etc. becomes heightened as a result as well.

274

This is a real long term gift that will keep on giving as now also Energy EFTers can begin to track and understand the connections between energy body problems and how these manifest through the physical body.

Energy Body Stress & Creating Stress Free EFT Sessions

The final gift of EMO to EFT is the realisation that energy body stress de-stabilises everything and to remove energy body stress first leads to much better and more profound EFT treatments all around.

Firstly, a stressed person is not in a position to describe their problems clearly. In Classic EFT this leads to endless rounds being tapped on "stress talk" instead of getting to the heart of the problem succinctly and in a logical way.

Secondly, to keep the client stress free at all times, by understanding that you "don't stop to treat the stress in the EFT session" but in fact, the stress relief is the treatment in and of itself, Energy EFTers now can build a safe, logical and stress free path into the heart of the problem. As the person is not just de-stressed but energized (going into the + side of the SUE scale), they become more capable, more strong and more powerful, thus putting them into a much better position to face the heart of the problem, even if there are extremely traumatic events involved.

The *strengthening* of the energy system and the *empowering* of the person through the rounds of EFT treatments has a much more powerful, logical and positive person arriving at the heart of the problem, and because of this, even "big problems" can then be addressed elegantly and more stress free than ever before.

In professional EFT sessions, it is not just the client who needs de-stressing; the practitioner has to de-stress too, so that the EFTeam is stress free and operating at maximum capacity. This was previously greatly overlooked and practitioners would be stressed, then reflect their client's stress back, leading to unnecessarily complications in the EFT treatment flow.

I'd like to mention also that as a homework assignment, to tell an Energy EFT client to simply tap on "stress" rather than trying to become their own psychoanalyst by trying to figure out meaningful

276

set ups and opening statements is far more successful and can really help clients gain a valuable life skill as well as something that is easy to do and easy to share with others.

Positive Energy EFT

Perhaps the greatest gift of EMO to EFT is that of Positive EFT.

In EMO, we learned that you do not have to go trauma hunting in order to help, heal or inspire a person.

Freudian entrainment has created a global situation where everyone truly believes that the only way to heal any form of emotional suffering is to go backwards, into the past, before you can be healed and go forward into the future.

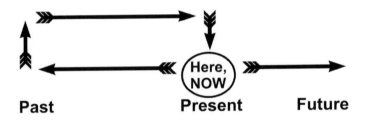

Past   **Present**   **Future**

EMO has proven that this is incorrect. The "trauma" (injury) exists NOW, it hurts, it is right here and now in the present. We can ask people to show us with their hands where it is located in their energy body, and "there it is!" By working directly with the problem erea, instant progress is possible; in other words, in EMO we go from here and now into the future, directly.

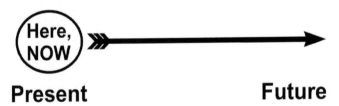

Present   **Future**

To translate this movement straight into the future from EMO to EFT, and thereby save countless rounds of tapping which may or may not ever find the "root cause" at all, Positive Energy EFT was created.

278

Positive Energy EFT or Positive EFT for short is a practice device to get people used to the fact that in modern energy work, you do not have to go backwards in order to go forward in life.

Instead of asking the old psychotherapy question of, "Why (am I afraid of spiders, feel so depressed, can't sleep at night, etc. etc.)?" and going on a long quest into the past, we ask, "What do I need to start feeling better?" and tap on that instead.

This keeps the eye on the ball, so to speak; makes testing easy; creates fast, practical progress and leads to the requisite healing event much, much faster.

- Positive EFT is a wonderful gift from EMO. It can be taught to everyone, including small children, very fast;

- Positive EFT does not require any prior psychology training as everyone knows what they like and what they want;

- As a first introduction to Energy EFT, Positive EFT always performs to give new people a powerful and POSITIVE first EFT experience;

- In every day life, it is far more practical to use positives than to have to stop life and go on a lengthy self-psychotherapy quest into the past before action can be taken.

Positive EFT, which is now taught as an introduction to and major component of modern Energy EFT, opens up the way to "The Oceans of Energy" we discovered in the original EMO research.

Even just armed with a simple Energy EFT protocol, people can become "Energy Billionaires" - because in the energy worlds, you can have everything, from natural energies such as tiger energy, sun energy, ocean energy to purely man-made desires, such as luxury yacht energy, king and queen energy, Lamborghini energy and everything else besides.

Positive EFT has taken modern Energy EFT out of the therapy room and made EFT attractive to the mainstream.

EMO's Gifts To EFT - In Conclusion

There are many more gifts from EMO that have gone into the new Energy EFT trainings; from working with events to energetic relationships (crucial in work with addictions, weight loss and groups) and from the new aspects model to understanding metaphor and the energy mind.

This really has supercharged EFT and brought it onto a new level, creating a next level on the oft cited "Healing Highrise" - we have made the leap from Classic EFT to modern Energy EFT.

So, now don't we need EMO any longer?

In the contrary.

EMO is the natural progression for people who love EFT. For some it may take two years, some may take five, some may take ten years, but eventually the very practice of EFT will be raising questions that can't be answered with EFT any longer and you then will need the more fluent and encompassing realms of EMO.

EMO at the advanced level and beyond holds a whole world of energy experience the likes we have never even suspected could exist at all. There are more advanced EMO energy patterns than would fit into a ten volume collection; and it is worth remembering that **EMO is primarily an energy research modality that allows an individual person to learn about energy in their own time and in their own way.**

There are literally no limits to EMO at all.

EMO will continue to produce patterns and techniques, some of which can be reverse engineered to empower other already existing techniques.

EMO can also be the engine that drives a revitalisation and modernisation of many other energy methods, systems and techniques; as the Germans say, "Alles flutscht besser - mit EMO!"(Everything works better with EMO).

In this case of EFT, I'm delighted to have the next generation Energy EFT practitioners out there now who have found the excitement and joy of EFT as energy work, and are discovering for themselves every day how much more fun, excitement and stress free change can be had when we drop the old limiting paradigms and instead step forward, rev up the engine and work with the energy body in this wonderful new way.

Blessings to all energists, and all who actively work to help people have a better with this life,

Silvia Hartmann

November 2011/June 2016

EMO and Events Psychology

Events Psychology is a clear cut way of working with important change events in a person's life in a clear cut and very direct way, which came about as a result of the experiences with EMO, Energy Psychology and working with memories in Project Sanctuary.

"Everybody knows" that a person who is afraid of a black dog now must have had an "event" with a black dog at some time in the past which caused that fear to come into being.

Even though "everybody knows that" it is not generally understood just how far and wide that goes.

Events are responsible for ...

- the formation of emotional responses,
- the definition of intrapersonal metaphors,
- the formation of beliefs, values and attitudes,
- the meanings of single words,
- all likes and dislikes,
- at the heart of every choice we make and every little or large thing we ever do.

Most importantly, events are not limited to trauma events.

In short, Events Psychology deals with four different kinds of formative events.

1. Trauma events that are perceived to have been bad and have negative repercussions;

2. Guiding Star events which are perceived to have been good at the time, but also have negative repercussions (as is the case with the formation of addictions and fetishes);

3. Unknowable events, which changed a person's life but they cannot say whether they were good or bad;

4. Missing events, events that should have been had but were not, and which are still being attempted to experience right now, driving strange and age inappropriate behaviours of all kinds.

All events have the same structure. Each event starts with an energy experience in the body - the event absolute - which is so cataclysmic, it changes the entire system in a heartbeat and transforms the energy system to a new state which may or may not be stable or perceived as beneficial.

This experience overwhelms the conscious mind and it goes off line for a short time; when it returns, the very first thing the consciousness thinks becomes like a powerful post hypnotic suggestion which will last until another event occurs to change that. These post hypnotic suggestions, such as, "I will never feel safe again," after a trauma or, "This is the best day of my life," after a Guiding Star event are called metacomments and they are the genesis of beliefs, values and attitudes.

In order to bring back evolution into these stuck systems, a new event is required; and until and unless a real event comes into being, such as the EMO Energized End State in EMO which is a healing event, the metacomments have to remain the same and will re-assert themselves.

Events Psychology is content free; and working with the metacomments with modalities such as NLP, hypnosis and EFT can bring about evolution.

However, the true place of power is the **event absolute** - the moment of the lightning strike which changed the entire system in a heartbeat. Something happened in the energy system that was most likely not completed properly, usually because the system had weak points at the moment of the event absolute and couldn't carry such a powerful charge properly in, through and out.

The rising energy forms hit a blockage, exploded and this causes both trauma as well as Guiding Stars.

When we go to the event absolute, "That moment when your life changed forever, where did you feel that in your body? Show me with your hands," with EMO we have the perfect, most direct and most powerful way to bring about an actual healing event.

A healing event is a real evolution for the person's entire energy system with the requisite cognitive changes as well.

When the event absolute changes, all the old metacomments fall like domino stones and everything changes in a heartbeat.

This is extremely powerful and wonderful energy work. It may sound difficult but it is not; by working directly with the body sensations and keeping the person's attention firmly on the energy movements in their bodies, we avoid all manner of problems that arise when people talk about their events with the conscious mind, flip into memories, bring out the metacomments and so on and so forth.

Here is an example of using EMO on an event absolute.

This person said that they went on holiday to Spain and something happened whilst they were there and they never really felt safe, ever since. They don't really know what happened, only that it was completely unexpected, very frightening and "from that moment on, the world was never the same again" (the hallmark description of an event).

> Energist: "So what's the problem?"
>
> P: "Since that holiday, I've never felt safe. I have anxiety attacks now and hardly ever leave my home."
>
> Energist: "What happened?"
>
> P: "I went out one morning on the terrace overlooking a beautiful bay with mountains, absolutely gorgeous, the sun was shining, I was so happy, and then something happened, I don't know what and I thought I was going to die, I had to literally crawl back inside on my hands and knees, close the

curtains, climb into bed and stay there. I have no idea what happened."

Energist: "The feeling you had back then, where did you feel that in your body? Can you show me with your hands?"

P (indicates a line from the belly button up towards the chest): "Yes something shot up, like being shot in the heart or something, stupid as that sounds ..."

Energist: "That's not stupid at all, that sounds about right. An energy form rose up and got stuck in the heart, it would feel like that if something like that happened."

P: "Yes I guess so if you look at it like that ..."

Energist: "We say it is only an energy, and that's a good thing because we can do things with energy. Where did you feel that being shot in the heart exactly? Can you show me?"

P (points to a location directly between the nipples in the centre of the chest) "I can feel it now, it is making me feel anxious ..."

Energist: "Take a deep breath in and out, and put your hands there, both of them. Your healing hands of energy. That's very good, that's exactly right. Now, take a deep breath, and another, and say and think, soften and flow, let's find out if we can get this stuck energy to move. Where does it need to go?"

P: "It wants to go upward but there's a block there."

Energist: "It's only an energy. Let's soften that block up, move your hands around and I help with my attention too. Soften and flow, and keep breathing deeply, keep your shoulders relaxed, yes, that's very good. What's happening?"

P: "I feel it's ... sort of elongating, stretching upwards ..."

Energist: "Excellent! The energy is starting to move. Let's soften it up more, and encourage the upward movement by stroking it with your hands, yes, just like that. Keep breathing and keep your shoulders loose, that helps."

P (wriggles and sighs): "Yes I can feel it going higher, this is most unusual ..."

Energist: "That's the reality of your energy system you can feel there. You're doing a good job, keep encouraging it, keep telling it to soften and flow."

P: "It's going up into my throat now." (swallows repeatedly)

Energist: "Let's make it even softer, more liquid, energy needs to flow like fine, pure clear water, soften and flow ..."

P: "Yes that's better. It's going up the back of my throat and into my head at the back where my spine is, that feels really strange, makes me feel light headed ..."

Energist: "That's great, now we need to find an exit point for the energy channel. It needs to go all the way out."

P: "It's coming over the top of my head ... oh, how strange! It wants to come out of the centre of my forehead, where the Indian ladies wear their dot? Is that right?"

Energist: "Does it feel right?"

P (smiles): "Yes, it does, it feels perfect. Funny though I thought things come into your third eye not go out of it!"

Energist: "We just go with the flow in EMO, quite literally. Now, think of that moment when the energy was rising up again, let's find out if it can go up that channel now."

P: "Yes, it's moving up quite fast, that swish around my neck and over my head feels really ... good, actually, and it's strange, I really have the feeling of having a bright light strapped to my forehead ..."

Energist: (laughs): "It's only an energy. Now, when you think about that moment on the terrace, how is that now?"

P: "It's amazing! I had a feeling as though I could lift up and fly away and at the time I thought I was going crazy, wanting to throw myself off the terrace and fall to my death! And I didn't want to die ..."

Energist: "And now?"

P: "Now - it's so clear, it was like soaring in my mind's eye, flying in a different way, I think I just misunderstood ... being free, being blessed with freedom ... can you understand that?"

This is a typical example how by working with the event absolute, the metacomments change free of charge as a direct result. New insights came into being and the whole experience is re-evaluated, bringing with it the additional energy, information and love, expressed in this instance by the client saying, "I'm so amazed that I could have such a spiritual experience, I never really thought I had it in me ... I can feel there's more to me than I ever thought!"

EMO is essentially designed to deal with emotions in the here-and-now and to transform those quickly and reliably into something better; however, it is also a perfect modality to work with major life events cleanly and quickly to bring about personal evolution.

People don't have that many events in their lives; indeed, one of the reasons that people are so susceptible to trauma and Guiding Stars is a general events poverty, brought about by the way we have organised our lives and societies so far.

EMO is not just a tool to repair past events and to help a person evolve beyond the stuck places these events represent; it is also a method of providing new events.

Any interaction at all, indeed any experience, no matter how mundane, can be transformed into a true event by the application of EMO.

This enriches us in the true sense of the word, but it also stabilises our events matrix by providing lots and lots of good events on a regular basis. When a bad event occurs, it is much less likely to throw the entire system into disarray; and also, the formation of dangerous Guiding Stars is much less likely.

Events Psychology, Silvia Hartmann, DragonRising 2009

EMO and Friendly Fire

Friendly fire is a term used for when someone is shot not by the enemy, but by their own comrades. We adopted this term for a common occurrence we observed that happens with victims and those who love them and want to support them; but not knowing how energy exchanges between people really work, it goes wrong and the victim gets in the line of friendly fire which causes even further damage.

The first time we came across this phenomenon was a rape victim who experienced intense shame, a burning sensation in their chest that filled their entire body with so much pressure that they used to cut their arm with razor blades and glass to alleviate that pain and pressure.

During an EMO session, the pressure was relieved energetically and the person exclaimed that they realised where it had come from.

After they had been attacked, they were interviewed by a policeman who got more and more angry and disgusted, the more details the victim was forced to reveal to him. The policeman had not been angry with the victim, but with the perpetrators; however, his broadcasts of total outrage, fury and disgust struck the defenceless, traumatised victim who sat directly in front of him instead and caused significant damage - new, further, additional damage - to the victim's already severely injured energy system.

Friendly fire in energetic terms happens all the time, for example when a child comes home from school and reports that they have been bullied.

Like the policeman, the parent will become outraged; but to the child, this outrage becomes a personal energy experience they have to make their own as there's no-one else there, and this causes further damage.

It also leads to "inexplicable" emotional entanglements and feelings of real guilt and shame; when friendly fire injuries have occurred, feeling guilty is correct and can't be talked or reasoned away.

Luckily, with EMO we can work with the energetic injuries sustained due to friendly fire directly and then, the guilt and shame are gone. In the case of the rape victim with the policeman, after the EMO Energized End State, the ex-victim said that they did not hold any anger or resentment towards the policeman who had been so upset and so angry, indeed, they admired the policeman in hindsight who really had tried to help and clearly was entirely on the victim's side; they just wished "this energy stuff" had been explained sooner so they didn't have to suffer so much.

There is a converse to this story, which is that when we find ourselves in a situation where we are the metaphorical policeman, and we get angry at the perpetrators, to EMO these feelings in, through and out as quickly as possible (see *Anger*) so that we don't inadvertently further damage the victims with friendly fire, and instead, help to stabilise them as quickly as possible after the incident.

EMO and Genius

EMO was materially involved in the formation over the past ten years of a clean and simple description of the structure of genius, what it is, how it works, and how we can bring our thinking up to genius level.

In EMO, we take the energy body seriously; but we also acknowledge that we know little about it and need to learn more.

There are some basic things we can notice, such as how emotions feel in the body, and some basic ideas which make sense, such as that the energy body has hands which are likewise, made from energy, and those would be the previously so mysterious seeming "healing hands" everybody talks about.

One aspect of conceptualising the energy body in this simple and direct way was to say that the energy body must have a head - and that would be the energy mind, previously known as the subconscious mind or unconscious mind.

The energy mind of course is neither sub- nor un- anything; it simply is there, a natural system that belongs to each person's energy body, and everybody has one.

When we start talking and thinking in terms of the energy mind, a lot of conscious contortions disappear and we are set free to start whole new lines of investigation and exploration.

EMO also gave us the breakthrough on the 6th sense, the sense that creates body sensations which have no physical origin. The conscious mind has developed a world map mostly based on just the information from the five senses which it knows about; the energy mind however works with all six senses and produces a far more inclusive and exact "reading of reality absolute" which is also far more information dense because of that additional 6th dimension of information.

291

Working with six factors instead of five creates a paradigm shift and demands a different form of language than the one we are used to; the energy mind communicates therefore not in words or two dimensional symbols, but instead, through visions - full six sensory lucid experiences, living metaphors as we call them.

These living metaphors are translations of an actual underlying data stream of pure energy; this is why it feels so good when a lightning strike of inspiration occurs, we shout, "Eureka!" and run naked through the town because we're so happy - an EMO Energized End State, by any other name of course.

This gives us the definition of genius - to be able to stream visions from the energy mind and create these data streams of information which are richer, denser and righter than consciously generated material could ever hope to be.

I have developed a system to encourage these energy streams and also, to control them so that people can feel comfortable with re-connecting to the systems of the energy mind that once seemed so mysterious and scary and were so little understood. This system is called The Genius Symbols, a Project Sanctuary derived process that is gentle, easy to learn, easy to do and lets anyone who wants it experience their own visions in response to their own requests.

As always, "everything works better with EMO" so if you add EMO to the process of learning and playing with the Genius Symbols, you can learn and learn to do much more, and much faster. Emotrancing the energy of the symbols themselves in, through and out, for example, helps to remove blockages and any existing injuries instantly and improves the clarity of the data stream likewise and right away.

The energy mind derived data streams which translate into visions we can consciously understand are extremely susceptible to stress; stress disturbs the data stream and causes "crazy visions" and extreme stress causes "Hieronymus Bosch style visions," so using EMO to relieve stress and blockages, negative beliefs and general

292

reversals to the idea that each one of us is born to be a genius and this is absolutely your birthright and mine, is extremely helpful throughout the process.

Finally, exercising our 6th sense to understand energy and to be able to feel it is of course a tremendous help at any time, and that of course includes then consciously understanding the visions from the energy mind and being able to work out more easily what they mean.

We have come to define these things and understand them the way we do now by working directly with energy, with the data streams that bring energy, information and love through EMO; simple as it may seem, by staying with the sensations in the body and focusing on the pure energy movements, we've come closer to understanding the nuts and bolts of how to engage human genius than it has ever been possible before.

So whether you are interested in developing your own genius thinking or not, this research and what has come of it proves beyond a shadow of a doubt that daily practice of EMO on your own feelings and sensations is well worth doing, and will bring rewards we didn't even expect when we first started out.

The Genius Symbols, Silvia Hartmann, DragonRising 2011

EMO and Home Harmony

Home Harmony is the EMO system for using what we have learned about energy to improve the energy flow in a room, a house, a home or a business.

The space becomes the body we are dealing with, where energy has to flow in, through and out without hitting obstacles, injuries or reversals, and the person whose space this is becomes the expert on the topic who works in direct consultation with a qualified energist or by themselves to improve the energy flow, to find the Even Flow for spaces, rooms, houses and so on.

As is the case with personal EMO, here we ask the owner of the space, "What is the biggest problem with this space? Can you take me there and show me?" The owners find it very easy to answer that question and will lead us to what is an erea which needs help. It is fascinating how the simple EMO style of thinking creates change almost instantly; it is easy and incontrovertible to notice where things become blocked up, places where clutter accumulates, places that are abandoned, places where things are that don't belong there and if they're moved, the energy of that space immediately improves beyond recognition.

By working with what there really - what the owner feels, and what we can actually notice and see in the use of the space and what objects and artefacts we find there - and by concentrating on the worst problem ereas first, big improvements can be made in the energy flow of any space right away. This additional energy gained then helps to move the endeavour along, making Home Harmony joyous and interesting, highly personal and appropriate, with none of the hard work and misery that was in the past associated with "de-cluttering" and no need to buy into an alien religion or philosophy.

EMO and Inspiration

Inspiration, or to inspire, literally means to put the spirit into something - put some energy into the system, by any other name.

People often think they are tired, depressed and listless and that they need to rest. The truth is that if you have something you find inspiring, and your are full of life, or full of fast flowing, ever renewing energy, you don't need to rest; and for the dull and listless, inspiration is the key.

EMO makes inspiration available to anyone who wants it, at any time, under any circumstance, anywhere, no matter what.

All you have to do to have an instant inspiration - read, an instant energy boost to your suffering energy body, like a vitamin shot in the arm - is to pay attention to something that is full of energy, such as the weather, and let the energy of that flow in, through and out your body until you reach an EMO Energized End State.

The weather is an excellent practice partner for inspiration. Many people feel depressed when it is raining or snowing, cold or dark and only cheer up when the sun is shining. Some feel depressed even when the sun is shining; but it makes no difference.

Dropping shields to the energy of weather and allowing it to really lift you, rush through you and "inspire" you in the true sense of the word is a powerful and instant anti-depressant that is available free of charge and without prescription at any time.

Weather energies are all different, but they are all pure natural energies and they are here and now, just as you are - re-connecting to the weather for an instant energy boost does more than just inspire you, it grounds you too in the here and now and brings you back to life.

There are many - infinitely many - other things and also people you can use to inspire yourself at any time, just for the paying attention to something and asking yourself, "Where do I feel that in my body?"

Many people keep objects - artefacts - around the house which carry inspirational energies. Just walk around your house and make EMO style love to your favourite things until you are filled with life energy again.

In essence, you should allow anything to inspire you - the food you eat, the water you drink can be a powerful inspirational experience when you open yourself to the water at the energy levels. Works of art, nature's works of art such as a single snowflake, a single raindrop, a leaf, a bird in the sky, there is so much inspiration "out there" it is awesome, and never ending.

All we have to learn to do is to bring it from out there "in here" - into our energy bodies so we can feel excited, alive, rejuvenated, and inspired.

EMO and Language

Language and EMO have three important relationships.

The first is the language we use in an EMO session, to describe the workings of EMO to another, or how we think about it to ourselves.

EMO works by paying conscious attention to our 6th sense, the sensations of energy flow in the body, and when we use the wrong words, the wrong things happen.

Please see the section on Language and EMO at the beginning of this book to avoid the kinds of mistakes which will seriously undermine the effectiveness of EMO, including the use of metaphor (EMO only uses the metaphor of water) and the use of the words "feel" and/or "sense" instead of the popular "imagine," which leads into the wrong modality and potentially into illusion.

The second important relationship between EMO and language is a part of overall energy awareness.

Energy occurrences are described in every day language, such as having a lump in one's throat, there's too much pressure at work, my heart is breaking, I'm stuck on him, a bad feeling in the pit of my stomach, she's doing my head in, he's spineless, she drains me and so on and so forth. When we listen with energy awareness and pay attention to these references, they tell us a lot about a person and also about ourselves when we learn to listen to what we are actually saying.

The third important relationship between EMO and language is that EMO shows us a new, reality based way in which to talk about our feelings to another person.

Instead of saying, "I feel invalidated by you being so inconsiderate when you should be emotionally enabling me ..." we say instead, "I feel a sinking feeling in my stomach," we open the door to a whole new level of interaction in communication.

Instead of talking about emotions, we demonstrate to the other person how we really feel.

This gives the other person the opportunity to do something about it; or at least to acknowledge the reality of those feelings which are real body sensations.

For many men, talking about emotions is a foreign language that they don't speak; talking about direct body sensations, using "Lucian's language" as we call it, they can express their states of being in such a way that it stays real and at the very least, their personal experience is acknowledged and validated.

It takes a certain amount of re-training, especially amongst people who have studied psychology, to stop labelling something as shame, anger, guilt, co-dependency, addictive behaviour and so forth and to start talking and thinking in terms of real ereas in the energy body that produce real sensations in the body instead, but it is worth it.

Practice the question, "How do you feel today?" and coach people to answer honestly and correctly, such as, "Generally quite bright but there's some tenseness in my chest, probably to do with the presentation I have to give in half an hour ..."

Especially in marital and long term work relationships, this form of **emotional honesty** can pay great dividends, especially over time as people start to appreciate each other's states of being, and may offer to help make each other feel better on a more regular basis.

EMO and Learning

We have already talked in great length about the fact that when energy flow increases, information flow increases at the same time and more is learned.

In that sense, every EMO movement is also learning - learning about yourself, about your systems, about your energy body, about your life. This should not be underestimated, especially as this builds up quite tremendously over time - you'll be surprised how much you can learn in a few short years about energy if you apply yourself and dedicate yourself to your own happiness with a will.

There are more specific and direct applications relating to learning, however.

The first and foremost are to deal with blocks to learning, injuries that preclude learning and also shields to learning.

I once met a fully grown illiterate builder who I thought was a very intelligent man. He however swore that he was stupid, based on his personal experiences at school where he couldn't learn or so it seemed. I looked him in the eye and told him it was his teachers who had been stupid. He said, surprised, "What, all of them?" And I held his gaze and answered, "Yes, all of them." There, something happened. His eyes widened with surprise and he started to laugh - an EMO Energized End State.

Soon after that, he learned to read.

Now this is advanced "conversational EMO" - I collapsed the shield that stood between him and learning at that moment but it's ok for beginners to take it slow.

Here is an example of a girl, 14 years of age, who was diagnosed with severe dyslexia. The EMO Master Practitioner has written the word, HORSE in big letters on a piece of paper and is showing this to the girl.

The girl physically shies away from the piece of paper, tries to force herself to look at it; her head is pushed sideways as though she wants to try and see out of the very far corner of her right eye. She is completely rigid, completely locked up, veins standing out in her neck and her fists clenched. She isn't breathing.

Eventually, the girl falls back into the chair, waves both hands in front of her and says, "I can't do it. I can't read."

Energist: "Where do you feel that word on the paper in your body? Show me with your hands."

G (holds out both hands, arms outstretched): "I don't feel anything but I don't want to look at it."

Energist: "Freeze a moment. Look at your hands. You've got a shield there, a barrier made from energy."

G: "Good. I don't like words, I don't like reading."

Energist: "How about we make a teensy hole in it, let some energy come in - it's only energy, you know, the paper and the words will stay right there on the table, find out where it hurts you?"

G (grimaces, shakes her head): "I don't want to."

Energist: "Really, really, really teensy? So small a teensy dwarf could hardly see it?"

G (smiles against her will): "Oh alright then."

Energist: "Point to where you want to make the hole."

G (points somewhere in a line with her nose)

Energist: "Ok, let that energy come in now. Just a teensy bit. Where do you feel that in your body?"

G (immediately holds both sides of her head at the temples): "It hurts my head, it hurts, make the hole go away."

300

Energist: (takes the paper off the table and hides it under their chair): "Ok it's gone. So you've got a real pain in your head, haven't you."

G (starts to cry): "Yes. But nobody believes me ..."

Energist: (gently) "I do. I can see it for myself. Look something has happened to cause like an injury to your head of energy. People can't see it but you can feel it. Shall we make it better, you and I?"

G: "Can we?"

Energist: "Yes. It's only energy and energy must flow."

G: "It feels stuck, pressing in, it really hurts."

Energist: "It would be good if it could flow away, become really soft, flow away like water."

G (sighs) "Yes I'd like that, very much."

Energist: "Ok, so this is only an energy. It'll move when you put your hands on it, you've got healing hands of energy, everybody does, and I help from the outside with my attention too. Ok?"

G: "Ok, so I put my hands on it?"

Energist: "Yes, massage the erea gently, take a deep breath and say Soften and Flow."

G: "Soften and flow." (sighs)

Energist: "That's very good. Where does this energy need to flow?"

G: "I think it wants to flow down, down my face."

Energist: "That's excellent. We discover the path and then it can flow away. So keep breathing and massage it, help it flow down. How is it going?"

G: "That feels really strange, like its sliding down my face." (Indicates with hands running down from the temples to the jawline)

Energist: "That's brilliant, exactly right! Keep saying to it, soften and flow, and keep helping it along with your hands."

G (swallows): "It is going down my throat ..." (swallows again)

Energist: "Move your shoulders and your neck a bit, that helps. Soften and flow. What's happening?"

G: "It's flowing down the middle of me, into my stomach. And down my legs." (wriggles her toes)

Energist: "Wonderful! It's going out of you feet! Where is the exit?"

G: "It's coming out of my toes, ooh that feels really weird!"

Energist: "How good are you? That's excellent, you did such a good job. Now go back to where it was hurting, how does that feel now?"

G (thoughful, stroking her jaw): "I can't feel it any more, not the way it was. Where did it go?"

Energist: "Down your body and out your toes!"

G (laughs): "That's funny ..."

Energist: "I've got the piece of paper with the word on it under my chair. How do you feel about looking at it now?"

G (takes a deep breath): "Funny I don't feel so scared now."

Energist: (gets the piece of paper, keeps it close to the chest, words down) "How's your head?"

G: "I can feel the pressure but it's ok, it's going down."

Energist: "Make it flow faster. Soften it some more. Say soften and flow!"

G: "Soften and flow!" (takes a deep breath, sits up in the chair, looks at the paper in energist's hand) "I want to see it."

Energist: "Are you sure?"

G: "Yes. Yes, I want to see it."

302

Energist: (turns the paper over, keeps it close to the chest).

G (leans forward, towards the paper).

Energist: "Do you know what it says?"

G (whispers): "I think it might be HORSE ..."

Now, we can't know from this one session if this girl's dyslexia was entirely overcome; or if this example holds for all possible cases of dyslexia.

What we can say is that there were some serious energy blockages in this girl's head and that she is most certainly better off without them. There was also a powerful shield protecting her from that which caused the pain, the words on the paper, forcing her to keep words at arm's length to avoid the pain.

Finally, there is the fact that someone listened to her and didn't try to explain the real pain she felt in her head away as being silly nonsense, an affectation, attention seeking behaviour, or ignored it, or told her that it "was all in her mind."

Without any improvement in her symptoms, that would have been worth it alone; do not underestimate the power of validating someone's personal experiences of pain and suffering which EMO provides.

This is a good example for blocks to learning, and how it is that any of us who are born veritable learning machines with a never ending ferocious appetite to learn more and more as long as we live, end up with feeling unable to learn something, whatever it may be.

Whatever it is that you think you can't learn, have no talent for, think it's painful to learn, too hard, that you don't have the brain for it, think it might take a lifetime and that it's now too late - take heart, quite literally.

Use basic EMO to take out blocks to learning, repair injuries in your system and have another go. Be prepared to be surprised how delightful learning can be if it feels good and energizing, instead of painful and pointless.

I'd like to add a personal note. At an EMO Conference, I conducted a short exercise on "removing blocks to computers" with the participants. It was amazing. People who were using computers every day were completely bemused by them, felt disconnected, overwhelmed, out of their depths, and many had huge, huge shields to their own personal computers.

Computers in the widest metaphorical sense are all around us in this day and age. They are in our washing machines, in our wrist watches, at our banks, in our TVs, in our sound systems, in our cars - it really does no good to live today and have injuries, blockages and reversals spooking around in our energy systems on the topic of computers.

Also, people with powerful energy systems who are reversed to computers tend to have a lot of mysterious "computer illnesses" from data loss to mechanical malfunctions - EMO your computer today and make computer misery of any kind a thing of the past!

EMO and Love Pain

Without understanding the flow of energy and the reality of emotions, love relationships and love pain when they go wrong makes no sense at all.

When we add energy work to the equation, love pain can truly become a thing of the past, setting us free to love much more, and love again.

Here is a story in the lady's own words.

"I've never been particularly lucky in love - when I was in my mid thirties, I fell in love with someone who didn't love me back but played me along, kept me hanging on for all the good things I could do for him. It was awful. It went on for a whole 15 years and it was miserable, so painful, I knew what was going on but I couldn't do anything about it.

"Finally, finally the pain got to be too much and I made the break but I was exhausted and swore I would never let that happen again.

"Then I found EMO and I used it a lot on that bad relationship. I believe in love and even though it went so horribly wrong didn't mean that I wasn't ever meant to find love.

"The day came and I met someone else, and yes, I fell in love again. And again, this man wasn't the right kind, he was married and it would never work, but this time I had EMO.

"Every time I got a huge wave of emotions, longing, jealousy, wanting to be with him, I EMOd it through. I kept thinking I don't want another 15 years of misery, life's too short and I really did EMO a lot, as and when it came up.

"Just two weeks and it was all gone. I was free and happy that it happened, it showed me I could love again, but I didn't get caught up as I was before.

"Now, I'm looking forward to the next time and I'm not afraid to fall in love any more. And who knows? With all that EMO, perhaps the next guy will be a nice one!"

What I particularly like about that story is the lady said, "I'm not afraid to fall in love any more."

It is certainly possible that we should all fall in love lots of times, and not just with marriage partners but with all sorts of things, all sorts of people. If we do it often enough, we might learn something about love, about ourselves, and even get to have brand new types of relationships that aren't built on need and desperation to own another person, but simply to gain additional enjoyment and additional energy instead.

If there is any love pain - old or new, raw or scarred - in your life, in your history, take some time and treat it with EMO. You will feel so much better for it and your body will thank you with additional health and well being, that's guaranteed.

Here is one more love pain story of many I'd like to share with you. This is a younger lady who tells this story:

"I was spring cleaning my apartment, moved back a side board and found behind it an old photograph. I picked it up, turned it around - the shock knocked me off my feet and I was on the floor, crying my eyes out.

"It was a photograph of my great love, the love of my life, and he had died.

"In amidst all of that, I all of sudden thought, it's only an energy, it's only an energy ... As soon as I said it I could feel the awful pain in my chest, in my throat, so much pain there, I remember thinking, no wonder I've been feeling so awful, so flat and lifeless ...

"I sat with the photograph and had my hand on my chest, saying out loud, this is only an energy, I want to heal that now, soften and flow ... over and over again and until it started to move. Then it did and then I remembered how much I loved him, how wonderful he was, how lucky I was to have known him.

"The photograph has a frame now and stands on top of the side board. Whenever I feel miserable or lonely, I see him smiling at me and I know there's love in the world, and that I'll find love again."

EMO is in many cases the only real the answer to relationship problems. This is such a wide topic, there is an entire book by EMO Master Trainer Sandra Hillawi on how to overcome barriers to love, how to heal injuries sustained in relationships and how to improve the flow of energy in all relationships:

The EMO Love Clinic, Sandra Hillawi, DragonRising 2007

EMO and Massage

The moment you switch on your healing hands of energy, any massage, any touch becomes different and has a different effect on the energy body of the person who is being touched - and that changes their feelings and emotions, and the entire interaction takes a threshold shift.

Using our energy hands in consciousness transform massage and touching, as well as grooming and self grooming, beyond recognition and as a result, the experience becomes different - more interesting, more energizing, more personal and more intimate.

The 6th sense of energy awareness adds an extra dimension and heightens the other five senses too when energy flow improves; this is particularly relevant for sexual touch and experience which is so important for physical well being, with the sexual energy circuits being the most powerful of all energy pathways in the energy body, and producing the most powerful 6th sense sensations as a result.

When two partners are EMO aware, and can help each other overcome reversals and blockages to enjoying their sex life simply by asking, "Where do you feel anything in your body that could get between us now? Show me with your hands ..." and massaging these ereas until the energy flow improves there, major improvements not just in the enjoyment of a natural healthy sex life can be expected, but also increased intimacy and increased energy for life as this spills over into the other areas of a person's work, inspiration, motivation and effectiveness.

There are many opportunities for people to touch each other with a healing intention. If you pay attention to the different ways people try and help each other with touch in times of crisis or trouble, you will see that naturally, people will touch a person's shoulders or their back, put a hand on another person's hand, or even take them in their arms to affect a "wordless healing" that is so often required at the right time.

308

With our healing hands of energy, which can become healing wings of energy and extend far beyond the limit of the physical reach, we can touch people with a loving or healing intention at any time. This the energy touch available in situations where physical touching is not allowed or deemed inappropriate; all that is needed here is for a person to be energy aware enough to notice there is something wrong, watch how the hands and body show us where the pain is, the blockage or the injury, and then stretch out their hands of energy with a loving touch to help improve the energy flow in that erea.

In the context of an actual hands on therapeutic massage, involving the client in the EMO client/practitioner dance is a wonderful thing, as Dr Teresa Lynch from the US discovered when she started to use EMO during her sessions.

She found that by asking the client firstly, "Where do you feel the most stress in your body?" and starting there, and then to ask the client, "Where do you want these healing hands to go now?" thus allowing the client to direct the flow of their own experience, tremendous improvements were being had. Clients also expressed their delight and how cared for they felt, how much they enjoyed the experience of being asked and listened to, to be given relief where it really hurts, and how wonderful it was to discover that their body could tell them what needed to be done and in which order.

With more energy aware clients or in the context of a real healing hands massage, the question that is asked becomes, "Where do you want these healing hands to go now?"

EMO and Meditation

People have strange ideas about meditation, often thinking it means sitting in a very uncomfortable position for a very long time and strenuously trying to think of nothing at all.

That is not modern meditation; in meditation, we turn our mind towards something we want to think of and experience.

You can meditate standing up, sitting down, lying down, dancing around the room and whilst walking; you can meditate by holding a beautiful landscape in your mind, or a crystal in your hand.

Entering a state of mindfulness and then adding EMO to heighten the experience, to resolve blocks and shields, soften and flow blockages that would stand in the way of a truly fabulous, orgasmic meditation experience is an amazing thing to do, and extremely beneficial for the whole person.

In guided meditations likewise, to be able to take an active role and work with the energy forms presented by the guide to make sure all flows smoothly and beautifully in, through and out, entirely transforms the experience of that type of meditation.

I have created some delightful guided meditations which are particularly suitable to energy work and which very much take the energy dimensions into consideration; and these produce many different kinds of trance experiences at many different levels.

I am constantly in awe of the human abilities to not just have all the wonders of the world where we are right now around us at any time; but also the additional ability to have the wonders of everywhere, and at any time, at our beck and call thanks to our conscious mind and being able to direct it at will anywhere and anywhen.

So if you are somewhere and it is cold and grey, you can close your eyes and remember a different landscape, something warm and lush, fruitful, green and sun kissed, and if you add EMO to the experience and flow those energies through your body in the here-and-now, your experience is transformed.

This is the kind of "instant meditation" that can be done at any time, anywhere, any time you need a boost; and it's not just landscapes you can bring to mind, body and spirit in that way. You can evoke people, animals, objects, existences - anything you need is available when we activate the truly extraordinary powers of the human systems that are not bound to what surrounds us at all.

EMO practice and energy awareness can make meditation into something so remarkable, you'll wonder how you ever did without, and feel sorry for those who don't know they can do that too. It's a superb resource for life, in sickness and in health, so I recommend it highly.

EMO and Metaphor

As we have discussed, the only metaphor allowed in EMO work is that of water in its various states of existence, from rock solid oldest, hardest ice to the lightest, finest mist. This is the only metaphor that works right with the instruction, "Soften and flow!" (as you wouldn't want to attempt to send moulten metal, for example, through an energy channel - ouch!).

By bringing all forms of metaphor in energy work under control in this way, and staying absolutely with the felt 6th sense sensations in pure EMO, we have finally found the way out of delusion and illusion in energy work.

This benefits energy work on all levels immensely.

Instead of "unicorn illusions of healing" we have real healing, and real evolution. Joy!

There is, however, real metaphor work as well.

As far as I am concerned, when a person starts using metaphor to describe a problem or brings metaphor to the table in the first place, we are actually dealing with energy work on a different level - I call this level of the energy body the psychic circuitry, the equivalent of the neurology in the physical body.

Using EMO inside real metaphor work, such as SuperMind, The Genius Symbols and Project Sanctuary, can and does completely transform what you can do with metaphors, which are also "only an energy" or data, displayed in the form of habitats, worlds, mountains, animals and so forth.

Here is a lovely example how energy awareness and an understanding of basic EMO can produce wonderful results in pure metaphor work (we don't call it that, we call it play instead).

This person had a repeating nightmare about an old house they had bought, and as they walked through it, they became aware that it

312

was structurally unsound, spongy, wet, rotten wood, the bricks being loose, walls leaning, everything felt unsafe and at the point of total collapse.

Now in a pure EMO session, we would have simply asked where they felt the dread as they were walking through the house in their body, show us with your hands, it's only an energy, soften and flow! and that would have been the end of it.

This however was a metaphor session, Project Sanctuary style, so here we enter the habitat of the old house with the person, we stand there, activate all six senses and ask the person where they feel that dread in their body. They are describing a "horrible feeling in the stomach that is really scaring me and making my legs weak." In this metaphor session, we remind the person that it is only an energy form, and if it finds its rightful place in time and space, all will be well and much will be revealed. The person says, "It wants to come out of my mouth, shall I let it?" Encouraged by the Project Sanctuary person, they allow the energy form to rise out of them, and it turns into a large silver bird that keeps growing and growing, until it so big, it shatters the house altogether and we are standing in a beautiful, calm, summer landscape, a wide meadow sweeping down towards the sea with forests either side.

The person is happy but this is not yet an EMO Energized End State; the threshold shift as it is known in Project Sanctuary has not yet been found. So the person journeys down the meadow to the water's edge, walks along the shore and there, they find a small boat ... and so the journey continues until a threshold shift is arrived at, and the Project Sanctuary equivalence of an EMO Energized End State has been reached.

This is clearly a completely different way of working with the human systems than the direct approach that EMO holds. Metaphor work is very complex and elegant, and it requires quite a bit of understanding of the language of metaphor and how things work in these shifting, ever moving worlds where energy is being translated into lucid visions and sequences of experience.

It is beautiful and a fascinating exploration of the human mind, body and spirit but it is not EMO, and anyone who involves themselves in metaphor work by any other name, using imagination and visioning rather than simply feeling energy in their bodies, is no longer doing EMO.

The golden rule for EMO is that you don't imagine it, you feel it in your body, and that's all we are working with.

This is direct, fool proof, can be taught to little children and to people who haven't even heard the word metaphor before in minutes. That's a very precious thing and to keep the simplicity of EMO pure, especially at the beginning, when energy awareness has to be re-learned from the ground up, is one of my life's missions!

- *If you love metaphor work, you will love Project Sanctuary.* ProjectSanctuary.com

EMO and NLP

NLP or Neuro-Linguistic Programming, created by Dr Richard Bandler and John Grinder, is a collection of modelled patterns to change state, thought and behaviour which draws on four original models, namely Gregory Bateson who specialised in communications theory, Milton Erickson who developed his own form of hypnosis, Fritz Pearls who was a renown researcher in psychology and Virginia Satir who developed new approaches to family therapy.

In order to let EMO take its natural place in Classic NLP, all we have to do is to take a video which features Virginia Satir in action, and instead of paying attention to what she is saying, to turn the sound down and to pay attention to what she is doing.

When we observe in this way, Virginia Satir's work becomes a picture book of EMO in action. She is constantly moving invisible things with her hands, manipulating ereas, drawing connections between people, encouraging energy flow, changing ereas that people show her and touching people with energy in mind. We can also easily observe how people react and respond to her direct manipulations of energetic realities. When we have observed this, we can turn the sound back on, and now the interlinkage with her energy work and the words she says come into awareness and we find the connection between energy, behaviour and language perfectly demonstrated.

There are many places where NLP deals with energy work without for the most part, ever naming it directly, and to make energy work conscious and real, EMO is a simple yet transformational addition to any neurolinguist's tool box. EMO brings the 6th sense to the party and fills in the missing and overlooked aspects to modelling; indeed, attempting to model behaviour without also modelling the emotional dimension, the conditions in the person's energy body, is simply doomed to failure.

315

Likewise, EMO expands, enhances and simplifies the concept of state, how to attain and maintain specific states and how structures in language naturally derive from different states which a person inhabits, and which start from the energy system out. EMO provides a clear methodology and even its own language which is generative and encourages personal exploration and the opportunity to learn in real time through direct experience.

It is my assertion that the energy body is the mysterious "deep structure" of NLP, that which NLP seeks to change.

As EMO works directly on the energy body, it is the perfect and long missing addition to make NLP techniques across the board more effective, more comprehensive and more complete.

EMO and Pain

We must remember that EMO is not designed or intended to work with physical illness, only with the energy body. This is the speciality of EMO and nothing is ever promised beyond that.

However, as we have observed, there are few experiences if any in which energy doesn't play an important if as yet undiscovered part; so when physical pain is an issue, we can use the rule of "Energy first!" to our advantage.

Physical pain and pain responses from the energy system are always intertwined; when we take out the energetic component, physical pain may reduce. Please note I said that it *may* reduce, we cannot promise that to anyone, and if it should happen, I regard this as a beneficial side effect of doing the right thing, which is to take care of the energy body just as fervently as we would take care of the physical body.

EMO doesn't cost anything and it doesn't take long; so there is no harm in asking the basic EMO question of, "Where do I feel this pain in my body?" followed by, "Where does that energy need to go?" and the instruction, "Soften and flow the energy!"

In most cases, "something" moves, and this something is the energy part of the intertwinement. With the energy body flowing freely again, there is less stress on the person's system overall and that's a good thing. What is left can then be treated by physical means and that's doing the right thing for the right level of the human totality as well.

In this way, EMO and physical healing do not get in each other's way; they don't compete with each other, they're not at war, neither is better than the other, and both can be dealt with as equally important for a successful and proper, full level healing.

EMO and People

EMO is a simple technique to help people deal with negative emotions.

EMO works by focusing on the feelings in the body. Rather than talking "about" anger, sadness, fear, shame, heartache and depression, we simply ask directly, "Where do you feel that in your body? Show me with your hands!"

Now we know where the place of pain is, and now, there are things we can do.

We can massage that place with our hands, breathe deeply and encourage the painful energy there to soften, and flow.

We can physically feel something moving, something flowing down our arms or legs, from our chests or down our backs; these sensations "that have no physical cause" but we feel them in our bodies, those are emotions.

You can't flow away anger, but you can soften and flow that feeling in your chest directly that doesn't have a name at all, that is a sensation, a pressure or a pain; and that feeling responds to touch, and to our intention.

In Western World "psychology and counselling" touching isn't allowed; but even there, the presence of another who can encourage us to keep breathing, to keep focused on the feeling, get out of our heads and back into our bodies, and to really let those injuries heal and the emotions flowing away at last is a godsend.

But EMO isn't psychology; it isn't counselling, and it's not just for therapists and clients.

EMO is for people.

EMO is there so that people can help each other.

Simply, directly and most of all, effectively.

When you see someone who is upset, or crying, or holding their heads in their hands, or their hands before their face, you don't need a degree in psychology to ask them, "Where does it hurt? Can you show me with your hands?"

They can show you, and you can encourage them to massage that place, make it feel better, let it soften and flow. You can take their hand, put your arm around their shoulder, put your hands on theirs and help with the healing.

You can let your desire to help the other flow from you like a powerful wave that helps the process of healing old injuries and flowing away the pain.

It's easy, and it is completely natural to all human beings.

We all feel emotional pain, and our own healing hands and those of others make the all the difference.

EMO is absolutely real, it really works, and you cannot go wrong with it.

It is so easy and so simple, it takes literally only minutes to explain how it works to someone who has never heard of it before.

More than that, you can just ask, "Is there an emotion that hurts you? An emotional pain you wish that would go away? Where is that? Show me with your hands ..." and simply start the EMO process of putting your healing attention there, massaging that erea, and letting the painful emotional energies begin to soften, and to flow.

As soon as that happens, people are amazed. They are relieved. Then they are astonished that it should be so easy to change emotions, that even powerful emotions, old and painfully hard emotions do indeed begin to soften, and to flow right out of the body, and that you can feel that happening as it is happening for real.

And then, they are delighted as they find the painful emotion really has left their body, and they feel peaceful, good, freed up after being locked down and depressed by their pain. They can breathe again, their whole body comes to life again.

And they start to smile ...

There is a mountain of theory behind EMO, and oceans of different techniques, approaches and uses for EMO.

But we must never forget that EMO is really as simple as that.

We must always remember that EMO is for helping people finally have something that works to deal with our emotions in a new way.

And we must always remember that EMO is not just for the chosen few, the well educated, the rich Westerners, for the experienced or knowledgeable healers, or elders and gurus, but instead, EMO for all people, and so that people can help themselves, and each other with their emotions.

Simply. Reliably. And for real.

EMO and Performance

A long time ago, people who practised kinesiology noticed that when a person thinks strongly, "No!" their muscles become weak, and when they think strongly, "Yes!" their muscles become strong.

That is a physical expression of a reversal in the energy system, and a fascinating example of how when the energy system goes weak, we go weak - mentally, energetically, emotionally and physically.

In that weakened state, simple things become difficult; easy things become hard; and any kind of performance under those conditions is going to be fraught, disjointed, complicated, too much to bear, out of control.

When we talk in terms of performance enhancement, may that be the performance of a public speaker, a singer or an actor; or the performance of a lover in bed; or the performance of a skilled craftsman, or the performance of a world class sports person, or the performance of a manager, the performance of a school child in class or of a family father on holiday, the very first thing we want to take a closer look at are the moments when these reversals occur and the system switches from "Yes!" to "No!"

When does that happen? And where do you feel it in your body when it happens?

Teaching a person to re-establish the Even Flow after a temporary systems collapse has occurred will immediately enhance performance as they don't need to stay in that collapsed state and from there, try to continue to do good work which is structurally impossible.

With a little practice, and I do mean a little practice, one or two good attempts to find the right channels and get used to noticing the sensation of collapse, noting the body sensation, remembering "This is only an energy!" and then giving the instruction to soften and flow silently and without anyone needing to know what is going on, we have the answer to performance failure right there.

This has tremendous repercussions on the performer's self concept and levels of stress going into the performance. Knowing that there is something you can do to restore your functioning when something bad has happened is a huge, huge stress relief - and with less stress on the system, a collapse becomes much less likely.

This is the first thing to do in all performance enhancement, to work with the collapses first and establish the way to re-reverse the system as quickly as possible.

Then we can go on to find more precise areas of application; particular aspects of the performance which could do with improvement and we can work on those to take out any blockages, shields, injuries or reversals to those activities, testing along the way to make sure there is now Even Flow in the performance of that aspect.

As a simple example, golf players have different relationships to the different clubs they use; they may feel less confident with one type than they do with all the others. Improving the energetic relationship with that type of club so it becomes not just yet another club (that would be the zero point of peace which tells us we are halfway there) but in fact, a favourite club they love to use and which enhances their confidence in that aspect of the game is easily done with the basic EMO protocol.

When thinking in terms of enhancing any type of performance, mental, spiritual, intellectual, visionary, emotional, or physical, keep it simple. Sort out the worst disturbances first, stay with the physical sensations of the problem ("When you know you will have to use the feared golf club, where do you feel that in your body? Show me with your hands.") don't get side tracked and always go for beyond the zero point of peace and into the EMO Energized End State, where the energy flow is fine and fast, and the person feels really good about the performance and about themselves.

EMO and Reiki

Reiki is a powerful energy flow through the body, and most people's systems are going to have blockages and reversals and injuries.

When a person starts to channel the Reiki energy, and it runs into these disturbances, it can cause intense flare ups of powerful emotions, memory flash backs and even what is called "the Reiki sickness" - a healing crisis.

Learning EMO in conjunction with learning Reiki stops all these problems from happening. We remove blockages and heal injuries with EMO before we start channelling Reiki energy, and instead of being painful and potentially injurious, running the Reiki energy cleanly and powerfully through the channels of the energy body becomes a totally joyful and wonderfully uplifting experience right from the start.

EMO also allows us to deal with mental and emotional blocks when it comes to using Reiki with others. We have an EMO exercise where we strongly affirm, "I am the healer," and any negative emotional responses, shields or reversals are being treated with EMO so it feels good and exciting to be a healer. Likewise, some people find that their new found healing abilities to be a burden, as though they were now responsible for healing everyone and everything. EMO is wonderfully helpful to release these burdens - they are only an energy, soften and flow! - and let a person become joyful at being a healer and able to help those who come across their path.

Using EMO in the preparation for the attunement is also very important; it is of the essence that both the master as well as the student are experiencing the full EMO Energized End State which really unlocks the power of Reiki energy work.

There are more times and places where EMO is very useful in the practice of Reiki. Understanding emotions and energy and knowing what to do when a client becomes very emotional during a Reiki treatment, which is often the case, is helpful to practitioners of

323

Reiki. Also, many clients experience further energy releases and other strong emotions after the treatment, and to be able to help with EMO over the phone makes the healing process smoother and more enjoyable for all concerned.

Reaching the EMO Energized End State every time with every Reiki symbol is another advantage of using EMO to make what is a wonderful and very powerful pure energy healing modality into an even better experience, and definitely helps the Reiki practitioner and master with their own personal evolution and their own path.

EMO and Spirituality

Spirituality without energy is like a fish without a fish - you have nothing at all.

Spiritual practice is all about working with the personal experience of energy, about re-connecting to the all-there-is, to the Universe at large, and to have powerfully positive connections of love, energy and information with other people and higher beings too.

It is simply so that when we add the basic EMO protocol to any type of spiritual practice, be that Yoga or Karate, Reiki or Christianity, Buddhism or Rosecrucianism, it all starts to work the way it is supposed to work as described in the old scrolls, and not just that, it becomes incredibly easy and natural.

When we pay attention to energy and take out that which stands between us and the rest of the world, we become more spiritual - instantly, free of charge, as a natural side effect.

This is a natural and honest spirituality that is based on personal experience rather than on second hand information, and with the additional energy, information and love that increased energy flow gives us, we get to be very good at everything from giving a true heartfelt prayer to opening ourselves to our fellow human beings with true and heartfelt compassion, rather than a lot of make belief and hoping for the best.

The whole point about EMO is to make energy experiences, spiritual experiences by any other name, into a personal experience. It really doesn't matter if an individual opens themselves up to the great Creative Order itself and feels those energies in their own living body, or whether they draw in the energy, information and love an angel has to give, a prophet, a saint or a particular deity from their own belief systems, as long as there is energy, as long as there is love, what more could we ask for?

325

EMO gives us a perfect tool to restore our abilities to become the spiritual beings we were designed to be, and we need to be, because if we lose that connection, there is no joy in the world. Especially the practice of restoring the systems that may have been injured or never properly activated in childhood that go to having a personal, living relationship with God and all the higher powers in the Universe can go a long way to simply help someone live a richer and much more joy filled life, where being a unique and beloved child of the Universe becomes a living a reality in every sense, in every word.

EMO and the SUE Scale

The SUE Scale (Hartmann 2009) is an evolution of the old SUD Scale (Subjective Units of Distress, Wolpe 1969) which measured subjective units of distress on a scale from -10, being the highest form of distress or disturbance, to zero, indicating the absence of disturbance or what we now call "the zero point of peace."

EMO experiences showed us that actually, you are not finished with the healing or the evolution of a problem in psychology until the person finds themselves on the other side of the zero point of peace, in the dimension of the positive emotions and good experiences, and so we needed something new.

This is the SUE Scale, first publicised in Events Psychology, 2009. SUE stands for subjective units of experience and has the two wings from negative via the zero point of peace towards the positive.

$$-10 \longleftrightarrow 0 \longleftrightarrow +10$$

A real EMO Energized End State is a +10 which indicates a healing event has taken place; when that happens, you can be assured that the problem will never come back.

The evolution from SUD to SUE shows the difference between non-energy based approaches and the energy inclusive approach of EMO in a nutshell.

The move from SUD to SUE is an actual paradigm shift.

EMO and Wealth

Wealth creation and prosperity, materially being rich, financial freedom are personal development targets that have brought many people into our field who would otherwise never have become interested in human psychology and behaviour at all.

And indeed, wealth creation is a veritable smorgasbord of opportunities to apply EMO and to work with the energy of money, of gold, of numbers, of personal power, and general reality creation at large. There isn't a person alive today, from any civilisation in which money is being used, who doesn't have all sorts of strange reversals, blockages, injuries and general spaghetti junction type snafus in their energy system on the topics of wealth, power and money.

The most reversed amongst them will declare money to be the root of all evil, want nothing to do with it, and may proclaim this rejection as a sign of how holy they are. Still, someone will have to give them their bowl of rice, their sheet in which to wrap themselves; somewhere, someone along the lines had to have worked in the fields and slaved over a loom to make that so.

After dealing with the topic of human wealth for some decades now, I've come to the conclusion that a really wealthy (hu)man is hard to find at present. There may be one though - an EMO story was sent in by an Middle Eastern gentleman some years ago, who was feeling very poor and desperate how to pay his bills, walked through a bazaar and came to the corner where all the goldsmiths had their shops with their wares displayed in windows and open doorways. As it happened, the sun was setting, struck all that gold and the gentleman had a huge EMO experience as he opened himself up to the energy of gold, let it flow in, through and out, and when he was done he was delirious with joy and said that he knew he was the wealthiest man on Earth at that moment.

328

There are many, many very rich people who have become rich because of particular set ups in their energy systems, and still they feel poor, which keeps driving more and more acquisition behaviour in their case; many of these rich people are enormously admired and people make them into role models, strive to be like them, think that if they could be like them, then they would be happy.

As Kahlil Gibran said so succinctly, "But what of the man who fears his thirst when the well is full? Is this thirst not unquenchable?"

Fear does motivate extreme action; but it's not healthy. Fear is the inverse of love and when we feel fear, it is an indicator that there's something wrong with our energy system and we need to do some EMO, right away.

Indeed, if a person did nothing but work on their various incidences of fear by any other name (stress, anxiety, dislike, procrastination, apathy, unwillingness, all the good reasons why not, etc.) an increase in energy, information and love is guaranteed.

These are the three building blocks we need to be successful and to manifest material wealth as well as spiritual wealth.

We need love to inspire us to be doing something that we love, a type of work that suits us, that invites us, that really isn't work at all but something we would do even if we weren't being paid a single penny for it, ever.

We need information to be able to do our work the best we can, and to organise ourselves in relationship to our environments in such a way that the work we do "works well" and has many payoffs.

And we need energy to do the work we need to do in order to serve the cause we love - and all that together then produces real wealth across the board, wealth for mind, body and spirit, and a wealth of positive, empowering experiences which also manifests in financial freedom and beyond.

329

So this is my tip to develop into a really wealthy human being in that sense - use EMO to literally transform your fears into powerful, positive action. Use EMO to become inspired and love that which already love to do, even more to power you up. Use EMO to remove shields that stand between you and the most direct, simple path to wealth, whatever that may be in your case.

And after a good day's work, use EMO to take in a golden sunset to remind us that there's more to wealth than just having a big pile of money.

EMO and Weight Loss

There are many different levels at which EMO can help with the ubiquitous "weight loss" which has become an obsession in modern day culture and is thought to represent the holy grail of personal accomplishment by many.

The first and most obvious application for EMO are the underlying emotional read energetic causes for over-eating and under-exercising which is what causes weight to build up.

People have all manner of energetic injuries regarding their body image and their relationships to food, eating and elimination too and to clear those first of all is the first step to a healthier personal relationship with the physical body, which must precede all attempts at physical fitness by any other name.

Many people who suffer from weight issues have their sixth sense of feeling energy in the body, especially in the mouth and in the stomach, confused with their first sense which denotes actual physical hunger.

Energy shortfalls, such as attention energy from other people but also general energy nutrition, causes something that feels very similar to physical hunger; and in neglected children especially, the two would have occurred at the same time, as a baby is crying and hungry for both human contact and physical food, so they have become linked and intertwined.

The simple solution to that is to respond to anything that feels like hunger with attention and by providing additional energy flow to the energy body first, using the "Energy first!" principle.

If the hunger was for energy, it is filled at that point and all is well; if it was physical hunger, we can then go on to feed the physical body in a calm and rational way. When the two are intertwined, changing one will by needs also change the other; thus it is that people who follow the "Energy first!" EMO way to weight loss and

331

healthy eating report that after an intake of energy first, they eat less, and also tend to eat better quality food in a more mindful and less desperate manner.

As EMO can be applied everywhere and at any time, repairing injuries pertaining to self concept, self belief, body image and so forth as and when they become noticeable provides very holistic and solid support for a person. Feeling fat and feeling ugly, for example, are feelings - and we can ask where you can feel that in your body, and EMO it through and out to an EMO Energized End State which leaves us feeling perfectly happy and delighted.

EMO can also be used to shift powerful self beliefs and post hypnotic suggestions that can play havoc with a person, such as, "I have a slow metabolism," - "I only need to look at a cake and I put on ten pounds," - "I can't lose weight because I'm not a teenager any more," - "Weight loss is painful and takes ages," - "Losing weight is bad for my health," and so on and so forth. Speeding up the metabolism, for example, is a direct side effect of ANY EMO Energized End State - it happens naturally when the energy flow through the energy body increases, and people naturally want to move, jump and dance when that happens.

Which brings us to exercise in conjunction with weight loss. Exercise needs to be a full body experience which every aspect of a person enjoys. This is not the case with treadmills where the head goes away and watches TV, leaving the body to do something by itself, and the energy system flat and uninspired. EMO Energy Dancing is especially designed to re-connect the entire human totality so no level is left out, all work together to bring about feeling better, happier, and finding a better relationship between mind, body and spirit in the process. Energy Dancing also uses all of the body, inviting movements from every muscle, every sinew and beyond, from the smallest muscles around the eyes to the biggest in the neck and shoulders, all work together and are being exercised at the same time. This represents a whole body workout which can be done by anyone, regardless of their levels of fitness or how much weight they are carrying already; it can even be done lying down and will still produce movement, increase metabolic rate and bring forward movement towards that all important re-unification of the human totality.

Once the lessons of whole body exercise and how good that feels have been learned through energy dancing, a person can then go on to bring that joy of movement to swimming, walking, running and moving in general life, helped along by the energizing and revitalising effects of pure energy work.

The final aspect to weight loss is the relationship a person has with food in general, and with particular classes of food within that. Many people are needlessly terrified of sugar and fat for example, and this terror or disturbed relationship then translates into all manner of disturbed processes in mind, body and spirit. Getting a logical and practical perspective back with all manner of food types is of the essence for a healthy mind, and a healthy body.

EMO is also extremely effective in re-setting a natural relationship with foods that have become "comfort foods" and also food addictions. These are food stuffs which have become linked with certain emotional or energy experiences; when we work with the energy relationship between the person and that food type, they are set free to choose once again whether they want to engage with that, or not.

The most profound overall help to keep moving towards the Creative Template of a healthy body, mind and spirit overall is the daily practice of EMO - drawing in lots of different kinds of energies that keep the energy body revitalised, rejuvenated and the person feeling good about themselves and about the relationship they have with others and the rest of the Universe. With that alone in place, better health, better and proactive fitness and weight loss cannot help but happen naturally.

EMO and Writing

Not long ago, a famous UK TV personality set up an experimental program to help 10 year old boys with their reading and writing skills as they were lagging badly behind girls of a similar age and because this is such a disadvantage when it comes to any form of higher education and gaining good grades.

Four weeks into the program, he discovered that the problem was that the boys didn't know how to talk - and when you can't talk, then you certainly can't write, either.

The boys didn't know how to express themselves, how to communicate, how to use words to put forth a cohesive argument, and they all felt bad about themselves and very insecure in their communication abilities.

When we talk about writing and writing skills, which eventually lead to creative writing and specialist forms of writing, such as writing how to manuals, operating instructions, training courses, novels, poetry, film scripts and advertisements that really work, we have to start there - with the talking.

Naturally, talking and thinking become severely disrupted when there is damage in the energy system - when the words stick in the throat, or there's a fog in the head and we have nothing to say because we can't think of anything, our natural abilities to communicate break down.

In EMO we find that people who have just experienced an EMO Energized End State start to talk fast, fluently, expressing themselves perfectly well and have no trouble even explaining quite complex concepts in such a way that they are easily understood - even if they don't know long or complicated words at all.

Simply put, there is an Even Flow to thinking, talking and writing, and when this Even Flow is interrupted then we can't think, talk or write properly; it's a direct cause and effect scenario.

It is very interesting what happens to talking and writing when people soften and flow their various blockages and ereas away - the communication becomes smoother, richer, and it feels better to listen or to read what has been produced as a direct result.

Writer's block and also, talker's block which many more people experience sometimes, under certain circumstances, such as when it comes to chatting up a stranger in a bar, during a job interview or when called upon to speak in public, or when called upon to tell someone that you love them, is just an energy - it's only energy.

These blocks to being able to "flow" communication, language, words and to have this match what the circumstances require are easily felt by the person themselves in their body; but also, the audience feels it and it makes them feel bad just the same when they are on the receiving end of a communication that stutters, splutters and fails.

I recently gave a new author the suggestion to read out their writing aloud and to notice when anything feels bad, feels wrong, breaks the flow. So they went back through what they had already written and found the "blockages" amongst the words, then found better words to bring the sentence back to a good flow; and for their new writing, noticed when these blocks kicked in, do a little EMO there and then, so the new writing was flowing much, much better as well.

There was also another interesting side effect. This author decided, after using EMO to improve the flow of their writing, to add a prologue to their new book - a chapter that told the story of who they were and why they were writing the book, a truthful testimonial of personal experience that had been missing from the book up to that point and brought the whole thing to life - for the author, and for the reader.

Improved energy flow, wherever you apply this, leads to more energy, more information and more love.

Now I'm not suggesting that when the readers read the new chapter that they might fall in love with the author and the book; but perhaps they'll like both more now because of the emotional connection, that extra energy that increases good feelings all around.

Here are my top tips for writing in the flow with EMO.

Firstly, take out all your fears and limiting beliefs about whether you are a good communicator or not - of course you are, you are born a communications machine as all people are and all that stands in your way are some injuries, blockages and reversals you picked up over the years. Get your energy flowing brightly and smoothly, and you'll feel more than ready to communicate more - you will find you love it.

Secondly I would advise you to take some attempts of writing, and/or of public speaking if you have this available, as they are only different sides of the same coin, and EMO any negative responses you have - judgements, like this is no good; instant flare ups of psychosomatic pain, oh, this is so terrible; anger at the past aspect who did this not good enough; whatever you feel, keep it up until you are filled with love and compassion for your past aspects who tried so hard to struggle through their own energy reversals and did the very best they could at the time.

I think this is a very important step for every writer and communicator to take; it really teaches us where we went wrong, what we have to do to put it right, and improves the self concept immeasurably.

Thirdly, with all these energy blockages out of the way, and you start to communicate freely, look forward to your own development as a speaker and as a writer. I have been doing this for many years now and as my abilities with words and language increase, I am constantly delighted that there is more, more to be learned, to produce better communication across the board - and to gain more energy, information and love in return.

EMO and the X-Factor

Some people have it, some people don't - and nobody knows quite what it is, that extra special something, that indefinable something, that "Je ne sais quoi" that makes something Xtra-ordinary.

It's funny because "Je ne sais quoi" actally means, "I don't know what!" in French.

So, what is the X-Factor?

It's the energy body, what else would it be?

Some people's energy bodies are shiny and attractive; they work just a teensy little bit better somewhere and folk notice this - a "star" is born.

They find shiny energy bodies very attractive - here is energy nutrition, here is a people food we have been waiting for, here is something we need.

Sorting out your energy body so it flows better and starts to sparkle is the simplest and most direct route to "find new friends and influence people" if you pardon the pun.

Improving your energy system is easy - all you have to do is to notice when you're in emotional pain, and do something about it so you feel happy instead. Not exactly hard work, is it!

Practising your energy dancing, your energy nutrition every day; doing Heart Healing as and when necessary so your heart of energy shines like the sun, becomes like a lionheart that attracts others and marks you out for a person that is different somehow, more attractive than the rest somehow, even though you might not be so pretty, or so young.

Taking down shields to people and repairing the injuries that give us our prejudices, the chips we have on our shoulders, the daggers in the back that make us energetically unattractive also helps.

You don't have to run into the gym, dye your hair, buy new clothes or resort to plastic surgery to be loved and highly attractive; all you need to do is the best you can to have your energy system in tip top condition and evolving towards your own Creative Template a little more every day, and folk will soon enough notice the difference.

Having more X-Factor is the opposite of trying to hide who you are. This is not about pretending that you're charming when you're actually not; or being sociable when you actually hate people. Human beings have far more energy awareness than they know themselves; on the TV show The X-Factor (the UK version of American Idol) the judges are always exhorting the contestants to "be themselves."

Now the contestants are very confused by that, as they don't know who they are or who they should be to please the judges; but if we look at that the EMO way, we could be a judge on the X-Factor and tell the poor contenders, "Sort out your reversals. Watching you suffer on stage makes us feel very uncomfortable - look, I can show you with my hands where I feel pain when I hear you singing, it's right here!

"Soften and flow your blockages of your own pain, and when your singing becomes pain free, I too might start to be able to enjoy it, drop my shields to you and love you for the radiant being that you could be."

Some might think now, "Well I don't want a career on TV, what do I need extra X-Factor for?"

There are many rewards to having a nicely working energy system beneath and behind the physical appearance. Happy, shiny people have all the luck. They have all the friends. Opportunities abound and the world literally throws itself at their feet, have you noticed that?

If you're not used to being a shiny person yourself and rather think of yourself as one of those kids who sat in the back of the class, jealous and bitterly envious about the cool kids and all their seemingly undeserved good fortune, take heart.

I mean literally, take heart.

Take charge of your heart of energy, your lion heart, and do lots of heart healing, every day. No matter where the disturbances in your energy system might be located, when the heart of energy grows stronger, the whole energy body becomes shinier and you are ramping up your X-Factor.

You become more connected - perhaps at first to the weather, landscapes and animals that inspire you; and with each inspiration, you become a little brighter and more inspiring.

Don't look back.

Enjoy exercising your energy system and learning more about the worlds of energy. This extra knowledge which includes how the X-Factor works, how people respond to that, what it is, and that it can be yours by right of birth makes the world into a whole new wonderful place to learn and play in, to let new experiences teach us how to change our minds, to overcome limiting beliefs about ourselves and about others, and also to feel much safer and much more cared for as we begin to understand our unique place in the Oceans of Energy.

And so ...

EMO Energy In Motion: In Conclusion

Over the millennia, much has been written and said about energy.

The energy worlds - our Oceans of Energy - really do exist and really are a part of reality absolute.

In the past, only special holy people were held to have the ability to "know more and see beyond."

EMO has taught us that everyone who wants it can re-learn to understand energy and how it affects the human body, mind and spirit so very profoundly, from the moment of conception to the moment of physical death.

The energy worlds might be inordinately complex; but that doesn't mean we need something complicated to activate our natural, Creator given, inborn senses and our intelligence to make sense of what the senses tell us - all six of them, at that.

EMO is profoundly simple, and yet it is this very simplicity that allows us to use it in so many different ways, so many different situations and circumstances, and to help us attain so many different goals of personal development and human actualisation.

If there is one last word of advise I have for you, it is this.

Keep EMO pure, keep it simple, keep it clean - and you too will benefit from the extra information, the extra energy and the extra love you will receive in return.

I pass over the simplicity and elegance of EMO to you now, from one person to another, like one candle flame will light another. Please pass it on to the people you touch in your life, in your own way, in your own words, but don't stray from the very simplicity of, "Where do you feel that in your body? Show me with your hands ..."

Einstein said, "When something is simple, God is smiling."

I think that everyone who makes it their business to put to rights what once went wrong, to help bring about an evolution towards more Even Flow, really is doing something to make God smile - and the best thing is that when God smiles, we feel simply wonderful.

With my best wishes to you and all those you love,

Silvia Hartmann

Creator, EMO Energy In Motion

February 2011/June 2016

ADDENDUM 1 - THE EMO PRIMER

As we are moving forward into more new and exciting research and specialist applications, and as all original documentation on EMO has been created in the English language and primarily for use by educated, 1st World Westerners, I thought it was extremely important at this time to write down the basic principles of the theory and practice of EMO in the simplest possible terms, so that there can be no misunderstandings, and so that it becomes possible for anyone to learn about this new and practical system for working with the energy body directly, which has brought joy, relief and peace to so many already.

The EMO Primer is designed to be translatable without losing the spirit of simplicity and the logic and directness of the EMO way of working with energy. You can also use the wording as a guide to explain EMO to other people as directly and simply as possible.

The EMO Primer

By Silvia Hartmann

1. Emotions are very important.
Emotions affect our body and can make us sick.
Emotions affect our mind and can make us go crazy.
Emotions affect our thoughts and actions, every day.
Emotions affect our health and our relationships, every day.
People make decisions based not on logic, but on emotions.

2. Our human world is created by EMOTION and runs on EMOTION.
Happy people don't lie, cheat and steal.
Happy people don't hurt one another.
Happy people don't go to war.

3. EMO helps people feel better.
EMO transforms emotions.
That is what EMO does.

4. Emotions are feelings that have no physical cause.
People say, "My heart is breaking."
There is pain in their chest, and they can hardly breathe.
If you look at their chest, you see nothing.
There is no knife in their chest; nothing is wrong with their body.
But they can feel the pain.

5. People have a physical body.
The physical body has a heart and a head.
The physical body has hands, a stomach, veins with blood, many organs.
When the physical body is injured, people experience physical pain.

344

Physical pain tells us when something is wrong with the physical body.

When we step on a sharp stone with our foot, it is our foot that hurts.

The physical pain tells us where the injury is located in our physical body.

6. People have an energy body.

The energy body too has a heart, a head, a stomach, many veins, and many organs.

It is all made out of energy.

When the energy body is injured, people experience emotional pain.

Emotions tell us when something is wrong with the energy body.

When we have emotional pain and feel it in the heart, it is the energy heart that is injured.

If we feel the emotion in the stomach, it is the energy stomach that is injured.

The emotional pain tells us where the injury is located in the energy body.

7. You can't see the energy body with your normal eyes.
But you can feel the energy body.

8. When the energy body is well, people feel happy.
They have lots of energy.
They smile. They eat well and sleep well.
They are friendly to other people.

9. When the energy body is not well, people feel emotional pain.
They are sad, or angry.
They don't smile.
They don't feel right.
They get angry and annoyed with other people.

10. The energy body is not hurt by sticks and stones.
The energy body is hurt by energy.

11. The energy body cannot be healed with knives and operations.
The energy body is healed with energy.

12. We have healing hands made from energy.
The energy hands are a part of everyone's energy body.

13. We have an energy mind that understands all about energy and the energy body.
The energy mind is a part of everyone's energy body.

14. Our thinking mind can learn to tell the energy hands to start healing the energy body.
The energy hands, guided by the energy mind, will know what to do.

15. A person is very sad.
We ask: "Where do you feel this in your body?"
We say: "Show me with your hands."
Now we know exactly where the problem is, even though we cannot see the energy body.

16. A person is very angry.
We ask: "Where do you feel this in your body?"
We say: "Show me with your hands."
Now we know exactly where the problem is, even though we cannot see the energy body.

17. A person is very afraid.
We ask: "Where do you feel this in your body?"
We say: "Show me with your hands."
Now we know exactly where the problem is, even though we cannot see the energy body.

346

18. There is no sad or afraid or anger in a person's energy body.
We say, "It is only an energy."

19. The energy body is broken and the sad and afraid and anger
are the calls for help.
We repair the energy body.
When the energy body is repaired, the emotions are different.
Instead of sad and fear and anger, there is happiness and peace
and joy.

20. You know that the energy body has been repaired when there
is happiness and peace and joy.
We call this the Even Flow.
To bring back the Even Flow in the energy body is the purpose of
EMO.

21. We breathe in with our physical body, we take the goodness
from the air, and breathe out what we don't need.
We eat with our physical body, we take the goodness from the food
and water, and let go of what we don't need.
The energy body needs to take in energy.
The energy needs to run through the energy body.
The energy body takes out what it needs.
It lets go of the rest.
We say, "The energy needs to flow in, through, and out."

22. In our physical body, blood must flow everywhere.
In our energy body, energy must flow everywhere.
When the energy does not flow, we feel bad emotions.

23. We say: "Energy is like water."
When it flows freely, it is like fresh, clear water and it feels good.
When there is a blockage, you feel pressure building up.
The energy flows slowly like thick, dense water.

347

If the pressure builds up more, the energy becomes harder and harder until it starts to hurt.
Some people start to cry.
Some people get very angry.
Some people become afraid.
Some people get silent and depressed.

24. In EMO, we make the energy flow freely again.
We say to our energy mind and our healing energy hands: "Soften and flow!"
The energy mind understands what that means and the healing energy hands help make that happen.

25. In the energy body there are natural channels.
Energy flows freely through those channels in, through, and out.
When the energy flow is blocked, we experience painful emotions.
We find the right channels and we help the energy flow with our intention, with our thinking.
We ask, "Where does this need to go?"
We say, "Soften and flow."
We help the energy move through the right channels all the way out of the energy body.
When we do this, we start to feel much better.

26. When one person helps another person with EMO, we say:
"I am going to help move the energy from the outside, and you help move the energy from the inside."
Both people must want the energy to flow freely again.
Both people think, "Soften and flow!"
Both people want the Even Flow to be restored.
Then their healing hands and energy minds will go to work and make it happen.

27. Our thoughts have an effect on energy.
We can build walls and shields made of energy around our energy

bodies.
We do this to keep energy out that hurts.
Energy only hurts when there is an injury in the energy body.
This is like salt only hurts when there is an injury in the skin.
We must repair the injury first and then there is no need for walls and shields.

28. Our physical body needs lots of food and water to stay healthy.
Our energy body needs lots of different kinds of energy to stay healthy.
Our energy body needs energy from nature, and from other people.
Walls and shields keep energy out and that makes our energy body weak.
When our energy body is weak and hungry, we feel sad, lonely, angry, afraid and depressed.

29. We ask, "Where do you feel this energy in your body?"
Someone says, "I don't feel anything at all."
We say, "There is a shield. The energy cannot come into your body. That is why you don't feel it."
We ask, "Where is this shield? Show me with your hands."
Now we know where the shield is.

30. The shield is made of energy.
Our thoughts can change things made from energy.
We say, "Make a very small hole in the shield and let a little bit of energy come in."
We say, "Where do you feel this in your body? Show me with your hands."
Now we know where the injury is and why there is a shield or a wall.
We heal the injury.
Now we don't need the shield anymore.
The energy comes in, goes through and out.

349

The energy body is no longer hungry.
The person feels much better.

31. A person has bad memories of the past.
There are many bad memories.
We do not talk about the bad memories or the past.
We ask, "Where are you in pain today? Show me with your hands."
We heal the energy body.
The person is no longer in pain today.

32. A person has been in a war.
There were many terrible experiences.
We do not talk about the many terrible experiences.
We ask, "Where does it hurt the most? Show me with your hands."
We heal the energy body.
The person remembers everything that happened, but it doesn't hurt any more.

33. A person has been attacked.
They are very angry.
We do not talk about not being angry.
We ask, "Where do you feel that anger in your body? Show me with your hands."
We heal the energy body.
The person remembers everything but they are not angry any longer.

34. A person's child has died.
They are very sad and very angry. They are in pain.
We do not have to talk about the sad and angry.
We ask, "Where do you feel the pain? Show me with your hands."
We heal the energy body.
The person remembers everything but they are no longer in pain.

The person remembers the beauty of their child, and the love of their child.

35. A person was in an accident.
They had an operation to repair the physical body.
Their body looks healed but they still feel pain.
Doctors tell them, "There is nothing wrong with you."
We ask, "Where do you feel this pain in your body? Show me with your hands."
We heal the energy body.
Now the whole person is healed and the pain is gone.

36. A person has a terrible illness.
They say, "Heal me of this illness!"
We say, "We only heal emotional pain, not illness. How do you feel about your illness?"
The person says, "I am very afraid all the time."
We say, "Would it help you not to be very afraid all the time?"
The person says, "Yes."
We say, "Where do you feel that very afraid in your body? Show me with your hands."
We heal the energy body.
We do not heal the physical illness.
The person is still ill but they are not so very afraid all the time any more.
We have helped this person.

37. People say, "You have to be a great healer to heal the energy body."
We say, "Everybody has an energy body. Everyone has healing hands and an energy mind. Everyone who has ever felt an emotion can learn to do EMO."

38. People say, "You have to study many books for many years to heal the energy body."

351

We say, "Ask the person where it hurts. Ask them to show you. Ask them where the energy needs to go. Help them make it flow again. It is easy."

39. People say, "I have had this terrible problem for many years. It will take as many years to heal it."
We say, "Energy flows quickly. Energy is very fast. It won't take as many years to heal the terrible problem because the terrible problem is only energy now."

40. People say, "I need to keep my problem because it is important that I should suffer."
We say, "The Creative Order wants you to live well. We only restore the Even Flow. We only heal what was broken."

41. People say, "Why wasn't I told this before?"
We say, "We don't know. But now EMO is here and now we can heal the energy body so we feel happiness instead of pain."

42. EMO works ONLY with energy.
EMO does not heal the physical body.
EMO heals the energy body.
To heal the energy body is very important.
There are too few people who help heal the energy body.

43. A person with a sick energy body might not look sick, but their lives are not good lives.
It is very important for people to feel happiness and peace and joy. If the energy body is working well, everything in life becomes easier.
We can work better.
We can think better.
We can heal faster.
We can be better parents, friends, and we can help other people.
To be an energist means to help people find happiness and peace

and joy in life.
It is a very powerful experience.

44. The Heart Healing Prayer

I put my healing hands
On my heart of energy
To heal what once was broken
To make right what once went wrong
To soften and to flow
To restore the Even Flow
So that my heart of energy
can once again
shine like the sun.

45. You can do EMO for yourself.
It is easy to learn.
EMO is natural.
Children can learn to do EMO.

46. Notice when you feel emotions in your body.
Where do you feel your fear, your anger, your sadness?
Show yourself with your hands.
Pay attention every day to the emotions in your body.

47. Use your healing hands of energy.
Put your healing hands of energy on your body where it hurts.
Ask, "Where does this need to go?"
Say, "Soften and flow!"
Pay attention to where the energy wants to go.
Let it flow all the way through and out of your body.
The more you do EMO, the easier it becomes.

353

48. Let more energy come into your energy body.
Take a moment each day to draw the energy of the sun in, through and out.
Let the energy of many things flow into you.
Flowers, animals, stones, water, the earth, the sky, trees all have wonderful life energy.
People, music, works of art, angels are different forms of energy that feel good too.

49. Let energy burdens flow away.
Ask, "Is my energy body carrying any burdens? Where do I feel this in my body?"
Say, "These burdens are only an energy! Where do they need to go? Soften and Flow!"

50. Energy must always flow.
Sometimes people try to hold on to energy in their energy body.
This is very unhealthy.
Ask, "Am I holding on to old energy? Where do I feel this in my body?"
Say, "This is only an energy. Energy must flow. Where does it need to go? Soften and Flow!"
When the energy flows again, you will feel much better.

51. EMO is very useful.
You can use it anywhere because no-one can see it.
You can use EMO to flow away fear, anger and sadness as soon as it comes to you.
You can use it to heal the past.
You can use EMO to have a better life today.
You can use EMO to fill yourself with beautiful energy any time you want.
Even for a beginner, EMO makes a big difference.
With practise, EMO gets better, and better!

ADDENDUM 2 - LEARNING EMO

EMO is completely natural, and the basics are really simple to learn and to do, but the more you know about it, the more profoundly fascinating it becomes and the more you can do with it.

Here is the suggested EMO learning progression:

Study This Manual & Do The Energy Exercises!

You have already taken the first step, congratulations! You can read this book many times and depending on your own states at the time, you'll find something new and interesting every time. That's an excellent start and from there I would advise to ...

Practice EMO & Daily Energy Awareness

Practice the exercises, especially the daily EMO practice exercises, every day. This will help start you off to really build up your energy awareness.

Pay good attention whenever you can to how energy affects people and animals, how we can track the effects of energy everywhere - practice your 6th sense every day, it will make you feel better, it's good for your health and if you should ever find yourself in any kind of crisis situation, energy awareness and knowing what to do can save your life.

EMO With A Partner

Check out the EMO primer until it makes sense to you. Explain EMO to your friends and family and try some of the exercises together. You can talk about EMO and energy in general then and share ideas and insights. EMO is the 101 of modern energism and creates a great platform to talk about energy and emotion in a whole new way.

EMO With A Professional Energist/EMO Master Practitioner

Try a session with a certified EMO Master Practitioner. Doing EMO with an experienced and officially certified EMO Practitioner is a whole new experience. Whether you want to gain an insight into how a real EMO Master Practitioner helps a person release long standing problems to feel so much better, or whether you would like to try EMO to solve a problem of your own, we recommend you contact an EMO Master Practitioner in your country and request a free 15 minute EMO trial session. EMO works in person and over the telephone, and most practitioners will be happy to give you a free 15 minute trial session. You can find EMO Master Practitioners at GoE.ac

The EMO Master Practitioner Certification Training

There are many EMO workshops in different countries around the world, please see GoE.ac/events/ for the latest live events.

The live workshops are a great way to do practical EMO with many different people and on many different topics.

The New GoE Energy Trainers Program

EMO is a hugely successful and extremely popular healing modality - there is simply nothing like it in the world! Among the real benefits of EMO are the immediate impact on the way we feel and think; the absence of religious dogma which makes EMO viable to all major world religions without causing a conflict of faith; the sheer elegance and ease of use; the logic of the theory behind EMO; the fact that no touching needs to take place; the safety and comfort of the techniques; the way it empowers both client and practitioner equally; how EMO dovetails so beautifully with literally any serious and correct healing approach without conflict; that it is so easy to learn and not least of all, that EMO is so hopeful, pro-active, positive and joyful in essence.

All of these and the user friendly, simple techniques make EMO an excellent choice for any existing practitioner who has long wanted to include the benefits of energy work into their practice, but felt that the existing approaches were simply too esoteric, too complicated, or too off putting to their clients, colleagues and supervisors.

As a GoE trainer, not only can you share the progress and joy that is EMO with others who are helping people through the practitioner certification, you can also give advanced EMO workshops, and run courses and trainings based on specialist applications of EMO that are important to you and successful in your local community.

Teaching EMO is tremendously rewarding, very easy and as delightful to the trainer, as it is to the participants!

The GoE Annual Energy Conference

Come to the annual energy conference and share the joy of modern energy with amazing people from all around the world.

The Guild of Energists has members in 68 countries (2016) and we are at the forefront of the brand new "Third Field" - practical energy based solutions without hallucinations, nonsense or dogma.

Energy is real, and when energy is high, the entire world begins to sparkle. Check out this year's conference program at

GoE.ac/conference

Join The Guild of Energists!

Above all else, we recommend you join The Guild of Energists.

This is a vibrant community of modern energists from all walks of life who have one thing in common - we love energy and we are immensely excited by the benefits and potential that we find in modern energy.

Receive The Energist journal, join the discussion groups, get great discounts on events and monthly free energy information.

Sign up today at GoE.ac/join

ABOUT THE AUTHOR

Silvia Hartmann is a full time researcher and developer in the field of human potential since 1983. From an original background in applied animal behaviour which culminated in publishing The Harmony Program in 1993.

Between 1993 and 1996 she developed Project Sanctuary.

After working with the emergent tapping techniques from 1998 to 2002 in addition to her own research into energy exchanges between social mammals, Silvia Hartmann designed the EMO system to enhance energy awareness and bring logic into modern energy work.

In 2009, Events Psychology was published as a clean methodology for use in general psychology and energy psychology.

After taking EFT to the next level in 2011 with the new Energy EFT Master Practitioner program and the new Energy EFT Foundation course in 2016, she wrote "The Trillion Dollar Stress Solution" to introduce the mainstream to modern energy and the Third Field.

Silvia Hartmann is the President of the Guild of Energists GoE.

Living and working in the United Kingdom, Silvia Hartmann continues to research and develop methods and techniques that are practical, logical and elegant in order to make the world a happier place.

ALPHABETICAL INDEX